The Anatomy of Communism

The
Anatomy of Communism

By
ANDREW MacKAY SCOTT

PHILOSOPHICAL LIBRARY
New York

Printed in the United States of America

1198245

For Anne Byrd and Rebecca

Introduction

THIS STUDY grew out of the author's attempt, initially quite casual, to familiarize himself with Marxist doctrine and its relation to contemporary Communism. After reading the writings of Marx, Engels, Lenin and Stalin for a time, several general ideas took shape which appeared to explain a good deal that was otherwise puzzling about the subject. When an examination of a sizeable part of the secondary literature on Marxism and Communism revealed no discussion of these ideas and, indeed, revealed surprisingly little that was of use in understanding Communism, the author decided to add another study to the number already in existence in the hope that the approach that he found illuminating might prove helpful to others.

From the start, the impetus behind it has been of a practical nature. I have sought to explore the inner workings of Communism, to lay bare its anatomy, and to make my findings available to others. The study covers a good deal of ground, but certain limitations have nevertheless been imposed upon it by this practical purpose. Part I does not seek to treat all aspects of Marxist thought, but only those important for an understanding of modern Communism. Marx's theory of commodity production and his theory of value, for example, have not been dealt with, since both have been treated by able economists of a variety of persuasions and are, in any case, almost completely irrelevant to the main aim of this book. Philosophical issues, by the same token, have been treated only to the extent that they appear to contribute to this purpose.

The method used—a treatment that is primarily analytical rather than historical—was selected for several reasons. The analytical method is superior to the historical when the aim is to focus attention on the relatively changeless rather than the constantly changing, on the recurring elements rather than the unique. To have combined the two approaches fully would have called for a considerable increase in the length of the work and would have required a reliance on historical sources far less authoritative than those used for the purpose of analysis. It would, thirdly, have meant repeating historical information that is more or less common knowledge, thanks to the excellent work of a number of historians and biographer-historians.

The study is critical throughout but is, I think, fair. I have not wanted to endanger a strong case by opening it to the charge of distortion. In order to guard against unwitting falsification of any Marxist or Marxist-Leninist position, none but authorities of unquestioned standing have been cited: Marx and Engels in Part I; Lenin, Stalin and official Soviet documents in Part II. On the great majority of points the difficulty has been less in documenting the position taken than in keeping the documentation within reasonable limits. I have wanted to establish my points conclusively without taxing the patience of the reader unduly. I hope I have been successful in steering a middle course.

Nowhere in this study will an attempt be made to deny to Marx the eminent place among the thinkers of the past three centuries that is rightfully his. As a thinker he was bold and creative. This praise may appear a strange prelude to a critical treatment of his system of thought but it will appear less so as the nature of his insights become clear. Almost all of the important ideas in the Marxian system possess a kernel of truth. The trouble is not that they are wholly false but that they are only partly true. Marx, overlooking the limited nature of his very genuine insights, pressed them beyond their proper limits and thus transformed them into errors.

INTRODUCTION

Part I of this study—chapters one through four—shows that a number of the most important elements in the Marxian theoretical system cannot stand up under critical analysis. Part II—the remainder of the study—is devoted to an examination of Communism in the Soviet Union and sets forth, as has never adequately been done, the actual relation of Marxist and Marxist-Leninist thought to Communist practice.

A. M. S.

Contents

xi

Acknowledgments

In writing this book I incurred a particular debt to two of my teachers at Harvard. Professor William Yandell Elliott offered constant encouragement and Professor Louis Hartz gave generously of his time and thought while this volume was first taking shape.

For aid of many kinds I am indebted to Elizabeth Metzelaar, Barbara White, Jean and John Hennessey, and to my father-in-law, Professor John William Firor of the University of Georgia. My wife's contribution is in a class by itself. Without her help this book would never have seen the light of day.

For permission to quote from works published by them, I want to express appreciation to E. P. Dutton and Co., Henry Holt and Company, The International Publishers and Random House, all of New York City; C. H. Kerr and Company of Chicago; Lawrence and Wishart Ltd. of London; and Max Eastman who kindly gave his consent to quote from *Marx and Lenin*.

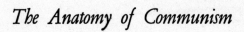

The Anatomy of Communism

The Marxian Psychology:
Its Nature and Implications

IT would be hard to find a better example of the way in which Marx transforms partial truths into errors than his treatment of man's relation to his economic environment. Chapter I will outline the Marxian view of this relationship, demonstrate its inadequacy, and explore the implications of this inadequacy for Marx's entire theoretical system.

According to Marx and Engels, man has no unchanging core; that which has been called the "essence" of man is no more than the totality of his social relations.

> This sum of productive forces, forms of capital and social forms of intercourse . . . is the real basis of what the philosophers have conceived as "substance" and "essence of man." . . . (Marx and Engels, *The German Ideology*, New York: The International Publishers, 1939, p. 29.)

But the human essence is no abstraction inherent in each single individual. In its reality it is the *ensemble* of the social relations. (Marx, *Sixth Thesis on Feuerbach*, reprinted in *Selected Works*. Moscow: Foreign Languages Publishing House, 1946, Vol. I, p. 353.)

The individual is not the master of his social life, but its creature. He is dissolved into his conditions of production. He *is* what he produces.

> In every society in which production has developed spontaneously—and our present society is of this type— it is not the producers who control the means of production, but the means of production which control the

producer. (Engels, *Herr Eugen Duhring's Revolution in Science.* New York: International Publishers, Printed in the U.S.S.R., n.d. Hereinafter referred to as *Anti-Duhring*, p. 326.)

As individuals express their life, so they are. What they are, therefore, coincides with their production, both with *what* they produce and with *how* they produce. The nature of individuals thus depends on the material conditions determining their production. (*German Ideology*, p. 7.)

Marx and Engels regard humans as wholly products of their economic environment. Before this view can be accepted, however, it is necessary to inquire about the mechanism by which they join man and economic forces in this intimate fashion. Their view is acceptable only if they can demonstrate the existence of a link between economic forces on the one hand and man on the other adequate to produce the causal relationship which they claim to perceive.

In spite of the importance of this problem for their theoretical system, neither Marx nor Engels ever devoted special attention to it. The general nature of the answer they give becomes clear, nevertheless, when relevant passages from their writings are scrutinized.

Hegel's dialectic is upside down because it is supposed to be the "self-development of thought," of which the dialectic of facts therefore is only a reflection, whereas really the dialectic in our heads is only the reflection of the actual development which is fulfilled in the world of nature . . . (Engels to Conrad Schmidt, *Selected Correspondence.* New York: International Publishers, 1934, p. 495.)

Hegel was an idealist, that is to say, the thoughts within his mind were to him not the more or less abstract images of real things and processes, but, on the contrary, things and their development were to him only the images made real of the "Idea" existing somewhere or other already before the world existed. This mode of thought placed everything on its head, and completely reversed the real connections of things in the world. (*Anti-Duhring*, p. 31.)

With me, on the contrary, the ideal is nothing else than the material world reflected by the human mind, and translated into forms of thought. (Marx's Preface to the second edition of *Capital*. New York: The Modern Library, n.d., p. 25.)

And dialectical philosophy itself is nothing more than the mere reflection of this process in the thinking brain. (Engels, *Ludwig Feuerbach and the Outcome of the Classical German Philosophy*, reprinted in Marx, *Selected Works*, Vol. I, p. 360.)

We comprehended the concepts in our heads once more materialistically—as images of real things . . . (*Ibid.*, p. 384.)

Thereby the dialectic of the concept itself became merely the conscious reflex of the dialectical motion of the real world. (*Ibid.*, p. 384.)

All religion, however, is nothing but the fantastic reflection in men's minds of those external forces which control their daily life, a reflection in which the terrestrial forces assume the form of supernatural forces. (*Anti-Duhring*, p. 353.)

. . . the appearance only of the relations of production mirrors itself in the brain of the capitalist. (*Capital*, Vol. I, p. 602.)

The key conception here is obviously that of "reflection." When the word itself does not appear its place is taken by a term which conveys the same idea, such as "image" or "reflex." Marx and Engels held that there are, on the one hand, "objective conditions," and, on the other hand, thoughts or images in men's minds which are the "reflection" of these objective conditions. It is this idea of "reflection," then, that Marx and Engels proffer as the link between men's thoughts and actions and the social conditions which are supposed to determine them.

The reflection theory is the only explanation they offer at this crucial point, but it is not a real explanation at all. Nowhere have Marx and Engels sought to show in detail how this process of "reflection" is supposed to work. What, for example, is an "objective condition" and what is not? How, out of the infinite number of objective conditions that must exist, are the ones to be reflected chosen? Having once determined what conditions to reflect, how does the mind know what thoughts or actions *are* the proper reflections of those particular conditions?

Marx and Engels not only failed to answer questions such as these, but, more significantly, they never sought to answer them. They never tried to explain how this process of reflection worked because they did not believe it required an explanation. On this question, so central to their whole theory, they accepted an analogy—the analogy of a mirror—in lieu of an actual explanation of human behavior. They assumed that men could "reflect" objective conditions as mirrors reflect objects placed in front of them.

If this analogy is accepted, all questions concerning the process by which the reflection takes place immediately become irrelevant and the gap between economic conditions and the actions presumably determined by them appears to have been bridged. The analogy is faulty, however, and its removal shows the gap never to have been bridged at all. Humans are not mirrors, and any attempt to explain the enormous complexity of human behavior solely in terms of this analogy must necessarily be misleading. It is sometimes helpful to think of an act as "reflecting" a given situation but it must always be remembered that an analogy is being used and that the notion of reflection does not explain the relationship involved, and does not refer to any known psychological mechanism.

THE MARXIAN PSYCHOLOGY

By treating humans as wholly passive reflectors of conditions external to them Marx ignores the problems created by the existence of a multiplicity of objective conditions and a multiplicity of ways in which each of these conditions might be reflected. He ignores, that is, the selective role implied for the middle term, the human being, when the notion of reflection is applied to human behavior. A mirror need only reflect, but Marx expects humans (1) to select certain conditions, (2) to determine in some fashion or other the thoughts and actions appropriate to those conditions, (3) to have those thoughts and perform those actions. A process of transformation is involved here that no mirror is capable of effecting. It is as if, perhaps, a machine were placed in front of a mirror and the mirror were then expected to comment on the efficiency of its system of lubrication.

These observations are of more than merely academic interest. When the implications of the collapse of the Marxian reflection theory of psychology are examined, it is evident that virtually every part of the theoretical structure is affected. With its collapse the famed doctrine of "ideology" is laid low.

> Your very ideas are but the outgrowth of the conditions of your bourgeois production and bourgeois property . . . (*Communist Manifesto*, reprinted in *Capital, The Communist Manifesto and Other Writings of Karl Marx*, New York: The Modern Library, 1932, p. 338.)
>
> The mode of production of material life determines the social, political, and intellectual life process in general. (Marx, Preface to *A Contribution to the Critique of Political Economy*, reprinted in *Selected Works*, Vol. I, p. 300.)
>
> What else does the history of ideas prove than that intellectual production changes in character in proportion as material production is changed? (*Communist Manifesto*, p. 341.)

[5]

Since Marx cannot demonstrate the existence of any mechanism joining conditions of production and beliefs in a one-to-one relationship, his assumption that the former invariably determine the latter is unproved. In the first passage quoted above Marx and Engels use the term "outgrowth" instead of "reflection" to effect the juncture but the main concept is unchanged. For one analogy, a second, equally vague and unsatisfactory, is substituted.

Along with the conception of "ideology," the Marxian conception of "superstructure" also collapses.

> . . . therefore the economic structure of society always forms the real basis from which, in the last analysis, is to be explained the whole superstructure of legal and political institutions, as well as of the religious, philosophical, and other conceptions of each historical period. (*Anti-Duhring*, p. 33.)

> Assume a particular state of development in the productive forces of man and you will get a particular form of commerce and consumption. Assume particular stages of development in production, commerce and consumption and you will have a corresponding social order, a corresponding organisation of the family and of the ranks and classes, in a word a corresponding civil society. (Marx to P. V. Annenkov, *Selected Correspondence*, p. 7.)

Since Marx cannot show that men's thoughts and actions are determined by their conditions of production, and since the institutions of a society would have no existence but for the thoughts and actions of men, Marx's assertion that the institutional superstructure of society is determined by the existing conditions of production must be rejected. Until Marxists can do more than merely assert that all elements in a society are one-sidedly determined by the "economic factor" it is no more necessary to accept their formulation than any of a number of others that might be advanced.

Marx has succeeded in showing neither that ideas nor that

institutions are determined by the "conditions of production." Yet it is this that he must demonstrate if his theoretical structure is to stand. It is by no means sufficient for him to show that they are "conditioned" or "influenced" by the conditions of production, or that they can be correlated with those conditions, since that is not the point at issue. The influence of the economic factor is not challenged. What is challenged is the way in which Marx argues from influence, which is obvious, to the presumption of cause, which is far from obvious.

The notion of superstructure plays an important part in the Marxian conception of history. Its removal cripples that conception.

> . . . In the social production of their life, men enter into definite relations that are indispensable and independent of their will; these relations of production correspond to a definite stage of development of their material forces of production. The sum total of these relations of production constitutes the economic structure of society—the real foundation, on which rises a legal and political superstructure and to which correspond definite forms of social consciousness. . . . With the change of the economic foundation the entire immense superstructure is more or less rapidly transformed. (Preface to *A Contribution to the Critique of Political Economy*, reprinted in Marx, *Selected Works*, Vol. I, pp. 300-301.)

According to the Marxian view, the economic "substructure" of society develops independently and as it changes the entire "superstructure" of society is forced to change in a corresponding and proportional fashion. Since Marx can only show that the "superstructure" is influenced by the economic "substructure" rather than determined by it, his entire one-sided theory of social change must be rejected.

In his accounts of major historical change Marx focuses his attention not on human actions but on the movement of certain great categories and abstractions. The concepts he uses are "forces of production," "relations of production," "means of production," "mode of production," "mode of appropriation," "relations of property," "relations of exchange," "conditions of production," "instruments of production," "conditions of property," "conditions of society," Capital, Modern Industry, Proletariat, Bourgeoisie, and so on. History, in the Marxian view, is a ballet in which these great, ghostly categories dance to the dialectical music of the universe. They "rebel," "conflict," and "contradict" one another, and in the process generate history.

If human actions reflected the movement of these abstractions, Marx and Engels would be justified in slighting human behaviour in favor of them. If the development of these entities provided the cause of which human behavior is merely the result, then the Marxian bypassing of human behavior would be warranted. Since, however, men's actions are not simple "reflections" of anything, let alone of these abstractions, Marx's preoccupation with them creates a gap between his theories and reality.

Classes, according to the Marxian account, are products of economic conditions, precisely as are all other elements of society.

> The new facts made imperative a new examination of all past history, and then it was seen that *all* past history was the history of class struggles, that these warring classes of society are always the product of the modes of production and exchange, in a word, of the *economic* conditions of their time . . . (*Anti-Duhring*, pp. 32-33.)

> Bourgeoisie and proletariat both arose in consequence of a transformation of the economic conditions, more precisely, of the mode of production. (Engels, *Ludwig Feuerbach and The Outcome of Classical German Philosophy*, reprinted in Marx, *Selected Works*, Vol. I, pp. 390-391.)

Since Marx and Engels cannot show that men as individuals are compelled to "reflect" objective economic conditions, they are further unable to show that "classes" are a reflection of these same economic conditions. Thus the Marxian conception of "class" must also be rejected. The role played by the notion of "class" in the Marxian scheme is so important, however, that the idea merits a more detailed examination.

CHAPTER II

Class: Reality and Ideal

THE INDIVIDUALS making up an aggregate may be placed in any number of categories depending on the nature of the criteria used by the observer: nationality, sex, amount of income, source of income, type of livelihood engaged in, position in the community and so on. It was not this that Marx meant by "class," however. He did not regard his "proletariat" and "bourgeoisie" merely as the results of a criterion arbitrarily selected by himself and applied to contemporary society. To him there were not four, seven, or ten classes depending on the preference of the observer and the criteria used, but a definitely ascertainable number of classes.

> Our epoch, the epoch of the bourgeoisie, possesses, however, this distinctive feature; it has simplified the class antagonisms. Society as a whole is more and more splitting up into two great hostile camps, into two great classes directly facing each other: Bourgeoisie and Proletariat. (*Communist Manifesto*, p. 322.)

In Marx's eyes these "classes" were fundamental social realities. He saw them as reflecting contradictions in the economic process itself. History was nothing more than the history of the struggles of these classes. "The history of all hitherto existing society is the history of class struggles." (*Communist Manifesto*, p. 321.)

Marx is saying far more than that society can conveniently be divided into those who are rich and those who are poor and that much in history becomes comprehensible when it is realized that many among the wealthy have in the past tended to exploit the poor, and that the poor have, on the whole, resented this exploitation. He is saying instead that societies are divided into two *clear-cut groups*, the oppressors on the one hand and the oppressed on the other, and that these two groups, as groups, must war upon one another.

> Freeman and slave, patrician and plebeian, lord and serf, guild-master and journeyman, in a word, oppressor and oppressed, stood in constant opposition to one another, carried on uninterrupted, now hidden, now open fight . . . (*Communist Manifesto*, p. 321.)

The two classes warring today, according to the Marxian analysis, are the "proletariat" and the "bourgeoisie." In order to understand what Marx and Engels meant by these terms we must first inquire, who *are* these "proletarians" and who are their sworn enemies, the "bourgeoisie"? First, then, who are the "proletarians"?

> In proportion as the bourgeoisie, *i.e.*, capital, is developed, in the same proportion is the proletariat, the working-class, developed . . . (*Communist Manifesto*, p. 328.)
>
> By the proletariat [is meant] the class of modern wage-laborers who, having no means of production of their own are reduced to selling their labor-power in order to live. (*Ibid.*, footnote p. 321.)

It is clear from these passages that by "proletariat" Marx and Engels refer to "the modern working-class," to "the class of modern wage laborers." There are, however, a number of other passages which shed light on the nature of the proletarian.

> The modern laborer, on the contrary, instead of rising with the progress of industry, sinks deeper and deeper below the conditions of existence of his own class. He becomes a pauper . . . (*Communist Manifesto*, p. 333.)
>
> Not only are they the slaves of the bourgeois class and of the bourgeois state, they are daily and hourly enslaved by the machine, by the overlooker, and, above all, by the individual bourgeois manufacturer himself. (*Ibid.*, p. 328.)

The proletarian is without property; his relation to his wife and children has no longer anything in common with the bourgeois family relations; modern industrial labor, modern subjection to capital, the same in England as in France, in America as in Germany, has stripped him of every trace of national character. Law, morality, religion, are to him so many bourgeois prejudices behind which lurk in ambush just as many bourgeois interests. (*Ibid.*, p. 332.)

They [the proletarians] have nothing of their own to secure and to fortify . . . (*Ibid.*)

The bourgeois clap-trap about the family and education, about the hallowed correlation of parent and child, become all the more disgusting, the more, by the action of Modern Industry, all family ties among the proletarians are torn asunder and their children are transformed into simple articles of commerce and instruments of labor. (*Ibid.*, p. 339.)

Our bourgeois, not content with having the wives and daughters of their proletarians at their disposal, not to speak of common prostitutes, take the greatest pleasures in seducing each other's wives. (*Ibid.*, p. 340.)

With the aid of these passages it is possible to discern certain additional characteristics of the proletarian and his position in society. 1) He is a pauper. 2) He has no property and no trace of national character. 3) His is a slave's existence. 4) His children are simply articles of commerce. 5) His wife and daughters are at the disposal of the bourgeoisie.

The essential point to be noticed here is the way in which Marx and Engels first use the terms "proletariat" and "proletarian" to refer to the *entire* group of wage-earners, and then, in the passages quoted immediately above, apply these same terms to a group necessarily much smaller. Comparatively few wage-earners could satisfy the conditions laid down in this second set of passages, yet Marx and Engels write as if these descriptions could be applied to all workers. By using the same term to refer to two different things, Marx and Engels tacitly identify the two. They suggest that *all* wage-earners are paupers, have their wives and daughters possessed by their bosses, and so on.

When it is asked, "Who are the bourgeois"? the same technique appears.

> By bourgeoisie is meant the class of modern Capitalists, owners of the means of social production and employers of wage-labor. (*Communist Manifesto*, footnote 1, p. 321.)

> No sooner is the exploitation of the laborer by the manufacturer, so far at an end, that he receives his wages in cash, than he is set upon by the other portions of the bourgeoisie, the landlord, the shopkeeper, the pawnbroker, etc. (*Ibid.*, p. 329.)

These passages define the bourgeoisie in terms of relation to the "means of production." There are others however that attribute additional characteristics to it.

> The bourgeoisie has torn away from the family its sentimental veil, and has reduced the family relation to a mere money relation. (*Communist Manifesto*, p. 324.)

> The bourgeois sees in his wife a mere instrument of production. (*Ibid.*, p. 339.)

> Bourgeois marriage is in reality a system of wives in common . . . (*Ibid.*, p. 340.)

Marx and Engels used the term "bourgeoisie" to refer 1) to employers of wage-labor, including "the manufacturer," "the landlord," "the shopkeeper," "the pawnbroker," and 2) to employers of wage labor who have wives in common, who see their wives as mere instruments of production, and to whom the family relation is a mere money relation. By using the term in this ambiguous fashion, Marx and Engels suggest, in effect, that *all* manufacturers, landlords, and pawnbrokers share these characteristics. Again they make it appear that what can be true of but a small number is true of many. Few persons satisfy the more restricted definitions of "proletarian" and "bourgeois" yet they assume that whole classes, millions of persons satisfy them.

"Class" is first defined in terms of an economic criterion, relation to the means of production. It is then assumed that the members of such a class will be united on questions of religion, law, morality and nationalism, matters that have nothing to do with this criterion. Marx and Engels appear to have overlooked the fact that applying a collective term like "class" to a group of persons does not metamorphose those persons but merely encourages the individual applying the term to focus on the feature possessed in common and to ignore all differences. The extent to which individual differences are ignored is revealed by passages such as the following:

The proletarian is without property . . . Law, morality, religion, are to *him* so many bourgeois prejudices. . . . (*Communist Manifesto*, p. 332.)

The modern laborer . . . instead of rising with the progress of industry, sinks deeper and deeper below the conditions of existence of *his* own class. *He* becomes a pauper . . . (*Ibid.*, p. 333.)

You must, therefore, confess that by "individual" you mean no other person than *the bourgeois*, than *the middle class owner of property. This person* must, indeed, be swept out of the way and made impossible. (*Ibid.*, p. 337.)

Just as, to the bourgeois, the disappearance of class property is the disappearance of production itself, so the disappearance of class culture is to *him* identical with the disappearance of all culture. . . .

That culture the loss of which *he* laments . . . (*Ibid.*, p. 338.)

It [the bourgeoisie] is unfit to rule, because it is incompetent to assure an existence to its *slave* within *his* slavery, because it cannot help letting him sink into such a state that it has to feed *him*, instead of being fed by *him*. (*Ibid.*, p. 333.)

The democratic petty bourgeois, far from desiring to overturn the whole of society for the revolutionary proletarian, strives for a change in social conditions which will make the existing society as endurable and comfortable as possible for *him*. *He* therefore demands above all a reduction of state expenditures . . . *He* demands further a removal of the pressure of big capital upon small by means of public credit institutions and laws against usury, making it possible for *him* and for the peasants to get loans on favorable terms. . . . To achieve all this, *he* requires a democratic—whether constitutional or republican—state constitution which will give a majority to *him* and *his* allies, the peasants, and a democratic municipal constitution which will hand over to *him* the direct control of municipal property . . . (*Ibid.*, p. 359.)

The italics have been added to accentuate the way in which Marx and Engels speak of "the proletarian," "the modern laborer," "the bourgeois," "the middle class owner of property," and the frequency with which such words as "he," "him," and "his," are used in connection with "the proletarian" and "the bourgeois."

When Marx and Engels describe "the proletarian" or "the bourgeois," they are not describing actual persons, but "ideal types." When they speak of "the proletarian," or "the bourgeois," or "the capitalist," they have in mind a prototype Proletarian, an archetypal Bourgeois, the Idea or Form of a Capitalist. These prototypes are then identified with *actual* manufacturers, wage-laborers and capitalists. A Marxian "class" is thus not made up of millions of different living individuals, but rather of millions of copies of a single prototype class member.

Marx's proletarian is an "ideal" proletarian and his bourgeois is an "ideal" bourgeois. Each represents a logical extreme. "The proletarian" is a person wholly oppressed, economically, physically, politically, socially and spiritually. The "bourgeois" in Marx's scheme represents the opposite extreme. He is the complete oppressor and exploiter.

Because each of these conceptions represents a characteristic carried to its logical extreme, using them to describe reality results in a vastly overdrawn portrait. The picture is done in black and white with rarely a gray to be seen. As in the old time melodrama, the villain is as villainous as words can make him, and the hero is completely noble, fearless and generally splendid.

Nor did Marx and Engels limit their thinking in terms of prototypes to "the proletarian" and "the bourgeois." There is a whole gallery of ideal types. In a passage already quoted a number of them have been encountered.

> No sooner is the exploitation of *the laborer* by *the manufacturer*, so far at an end, that he receives his wages in cash, than he is set upon by the other portions of the bourgeoisie, *the landlord, the shopkeeper, the pawnbroker*, etc. (*Communist Manifesto*, p. 329.)

> The lower middle class, *the small manufacturer, the shopkeeper, the artisan, the peasant*, all these . . . (*Ibid.*, p. 332.) [Italics mine, AMS.]

This thinking in terms of "essences" does not stop here, however, but is extended to such things as "*the* family," and, even more importantly, to "*the* state." Italics are added in the following passages:

> On what foundation is *the present family, the bourgeois family,* based? On capital, on private gain. (*Communist Manifesto*, p. 339.)

> *The modern state*, whatever its form, is an essentially capitalist machine; it is *the state* of the capitalists . . . (*Anti-Duhring*, p. 313.)

> But in reality *the State* is nothing else than a machine

for the oppression of one class by another ... (Engels, Introduction to the German edition of Marx's *Civil War in France*, reprinted in *Capital, The Communist Manifesto and Other Writings of Karl Marx*, p. 381.)

The concepts that Marx and Engels use have a good deal in common with the "ideal" concepts that physicists occasionally use, the perfectly rigid body, the frictionless machine, and so on. Whereas a physicist would realize that he was working with ideal conceptions and would not expect to find their counterparts in reality, Marx and Engels consistently identify their ideal conceptions with institutions and persons that actually exist.

When Marx speaks of "the state" he has in mind the image of an "ideal" state, a state having as its sole characteristic the function of serving one "class" as a means of suppressing another. In saying that "The modern state, whatever its form," has this as its principal feature, Marx and Engels identify *every existing state* with their ideal state. They assume that every state, parliamentary or despotic, new or old, large or small, European or Eastern, has as its central feature this class function.

> But in reality the state is nothing else than a machine for the oppression of one class by another class, and that no less so in the democratic republic than under the monarchy. (*Ibid.*)

Virtually every term used by Marx and Engels has two meanings: first, the ideal concept of Marxian theory, and second, a reality that in any given case may approximate the ideal conception to a greater or lesser extent but which is unlikely to coincide with it, if only because it *is* an ideal conception. Since Marx and Engels assume a complete identity between their ideal conceptions and reality, they move at every point from one meaning to the other without perceiving that they are treating as identical things which are different, without perceiving that they are identifying the real and the ideal.

The result is that a series of ambiguities runs through the whole of their writings.

When the words that men use become ambiguous, confusion can only be avoided with great effort. It can be avoided in this case only if the systematic Marxian identification of the real and the ideal is countered by an equally systematic separation of the two. At every point at which Marx and Engels identify one of their ideal conceptions with reality, a critical reader must ask what, in fact, the relation between the two is. When, for example, "the state" is referred to, it must immediately be asked whether it is some actual state, or the prototype state of Marxist theory that is meant. When "the bourgeois" is referred to, it must be discovered whether an actual manufacturer or employer of wage-labor is meant, or at least some statistically "average" manufacturer, or whether it is the perfect villain of Marxist theory. When "the proletarian" is spoken of, it must be asked whether the wholly oppressed, starved, tyrannized ideal "proletarian" of Marxist theory is meant or an actual worker or a statistically "average" worker.

The same thing is true when the "class" rather than the individual is spoken of. When the term "bourgeoisie" is used, it must be asked whether the ideal exploiting class of Marxist theory is meant, or the vast number of manufacturers and employers who actually exist and who differ from one another as much as humans customarily do. Similarly, the reality and the fiction must be distinguished when the term "proletariat" is used. The reality is that group of men and women engaged in industrial work, some of whom are undergoing economic and other hardships, some of whom are not. The fiction is a brutalized, enslaved, mercilessly exploited, thoroughly oppressed mass of identical "proletarians."

CHAPTER III

Freedom, Authority and the Class Will

MARX and Engels assume that an individual's thoughts and actions are determined by his relation to the means of production, are a reflection, that is to say, of his class position. Since they believe that there exist only two classes of any significance, they naturally divide all persons into those who adhere to "proletarian" beliefs and those who adhere to a "bourgeois ideology." The beliefs, ideas, and desires of the persons within each of these "classes" are assumed to be identical. Marx and Engels treat this assumed agreement as a single "class will."

> Your very ideas are but the outgrowth of the conditions of your bourgeois production and bourgeois property, just as your jurisprudence is but the will of your class made into a law for all, a will whose essential character and direction are determined by the economical conditions of existence of your class. (*Communist Manifesto*, p. 338.)
> And this moment comes as soon as the mass of the people—town and country workers and peasants—*has* a will. . . . What the bourgeois democracy of 1848 could not accomplish, just because it was *bourgeois* and not proletarian, namely, to give the labouring masses a will whose content was in accord with their class position—socialism will infallibly secure. (*Anti-Duhring*, p. 194.)
> Thus to the German philosophers of the Eighteenth Century . . . the utterance of the will of the revolutionary French bourgeoisie signified in their eyes the laws of . . . true human Will generally. (*Communist Manifesto*, p. 347.)

In passages like these, Marx and Engels explicitly acknowledge their assumption of the existence of a class will. More often, it is simply taken for granted, as in passages such as the following:

> The seizure of the means of production by society puts an end to commodity production, and therewith to the domination of the product over the producer. Anarchy in social production is replaced by conscious organisation on a planned basis . . . (*Anti-Duhring*, p. 318.)
> And when this act has been accomplished, when society, by taking possession of all means of production and using them on a planned basis, has freed itself . . . (*Anti-Duhring*, p. 355.)
> The appropriation by society of the means of production will put an end not only to the artificial restraints on production which exist today, but also to the positive waste and destruction of productive forces and products . . . (*Ibid.*, p. 317.)
> A similar manipulation of the productive forces of the present day, on the basis of their real nature at last recognized by society, opens the way to the replacement of the anarchy of social production by a socially planned regulation of production in accordance with the needs both of society as a whole and of each individual. (*Ibid.*, p. 314.)
> In making itself the master of all the means of production, in order to use them in accordance with a social plan, society puts an end to the former subjection of men to their own means of production. It goes without saying that society cannot itself be free unless every individual is free. (*Ibid.*, p. 328.)

"Society" is to seize the means of production. It is to make itself "master" of these means, in order to use them in accordance with a "social plan." We must ask, however, how exactly it is that "society," numbering many millions of persons, is to perform this act of seizing the means of production? What is this "social plan" that is spoken of? How are millions of persons spread over a considerable area to come together and draw up this "plan" for the direction of the industrial process?

From the moment when society enters into possession of the means of production and uses them in direct association for production, the labour of each individual, however varied its specifically useful character may be, is immediately and directly social labour. The quantity of social labour contained in a product has then no need to be established in a roundabout way; daily experience shows in a direct way how much of it is required on the average. Society can simply calculate how many hours of labour are contained in a steam-engine, a bushel of wheat of the last harvest, or a hundred square yards of cloth of a certain quality. It could therefore never occur to it still to express the quantity of labour put into the products, which it will then know directly and in its absolute amount, in a third product. . . . It is true that even then it will still be necessary for society to know how much labour each article of consumption requires for its production. It will have to arrange its plan of production in accordance with its means of production, which include, in particular, its labour forces. The useful effects of the various articles of consumption, compared with each other and with the quantity of labour required for their production, will in the last analysis, determine the plan. People will be able to manage everything very simply, without the intervention of the famous "value." (*Anti-Duhring*, pp. 345-46.)

It is important to notice the variety and complexity of the tasks which Engels assigns to "society" in this passage. It is presumed to be able to make intricate calculations, gather data, make comparisons, and ultimately to emerge with a plan which will state in detail the quantity of each article to be produced. After describing this process, Engels concludes that "People will be able to manage everything very simply . . ."

By the simple expedient of attributing mind and will to society, Marx and Engels overcome the enormous difficulties involved in trying to explain how these intricate tasks are to be accomplished. Thus in the passages above, society is assumed to be capable of cognition, since it is to "recognize" the real nature of productive forces. It is assumed to be capable of having purpose and acting on it, since it is to seize the means of production in order to use them in a particular fashion. It is assumed to be fairly competent at mathematics since it is to "calculate" the number of hours of labor contained in a variety of things like steam engines and table cloths. Further, it can "know" things, it can "express" itself, and things can "occur" to it.

The doctrine of the "classless society" and that of the "withering away" of the state become comprehensible only when it is realised that Marx and Engels thought in terms of a class will.

> The first act in which the state really comes forward as the representative of society as a whole—the taking possession of the means of production in the name of society—is at the same time its last independent act as a state. The interference of the state power in social relations becomes superfluous in one sphere after another, and then ceases of itself. The government of persons is replaced by the administration of things and the direction of the process of production. The state is not "abolished," *it withers away.* (*Anti-Duhring*, p. 315.)

What picture of society emerges from this famous passage? It is clear that in the classless society persons will cease to be governed; instead, "things" are to be administered, and the process of production is to be directed.

Certain questions immediately arise. How are "things" to be administered without at the same time administering persons? Since the "process of production" involves persons in a most intimate way, how is that process to be directed without at the same time directing or governing people? How, furthermore, can Marx and Engels expect the state to wither away at the very same time that all the means of production are to be socialized? Is not their demand for socialism completely at odds with their demand for the abolition of the state?

The failure of Marx and Engels to perceive the difficulties raised by questions like these seems inexplicable until it is appreciated that they took for granted the existence of a class will. Assume the existence of a class will, and these problems cease to be problems. Persons will not need to be governed in the classless society since, by virtue of the class will, they will be in agreement on all points and will always act in unison. The class will makes government superfluous.

If the class will orientation of Marx and Engels is kept in mind it also becomes clear why they feel free to call for the abolition of the state at the same time that they call for the socialization of all means of production. The explanation turns on their conception of the state as purely and simply an engine for the oppression of one class by another.

> In order that these contradictions, these classes with conflicting economic interests, may not annihilate themselves and society in a useless struggle, a power becomes necessary that stands apparently above society and has the function of keeping down the conflicts and maintaining "order." And this power, the outgrowth of society, but assuming supremacy over it and becoming more and more divorced from it, is the state. (Engels, *The Origin of the Family, Private Property and the State*, Chicago: Charles H. Kerr and Co., 1902, p. 206.)

The state is the result of the desire to keep down class conflicts. But having arisen amid these conflicts, it is as a rule the state of the most powerful economic class that by force of its economic supremacy becomes also the ruling political class and thus acquires new means of subduing and exploiting the oppressed masses. The antique state was, therefore, the state of the slave owners for the purpose of holding the slaves in check. The feudal state was the organ of the nobility for the oppression of the serfs and dependent farmers. The modern representative state is the tool of the capitalist exploiters of wage labor. (*Ibid.*, pp. 208-209.)

Former society, moving in class antagonisms, had need of the state, that is, an organization of the exploiting class at each period for the maintenance of its external conditions of production; that is, therefore, for the forcible holding down of the exploited class in the conditions of oppression (slavery, villeinage or serfdom, wage labour) determined by the existing mode of production. (*Anti-Duhring*, pp. 314-315.)

In the Marxian view the state has no function other than this function of oppression. The executive and administrative functions usually attributed to the state are, in the Marxian scheme, denied to the state and attributed to the class. Since the state apparatus exists only to serve one class as a means of oppressing another, it can be dispensed with when classes themselves disappear, without in any way interfering with the ability of society to govern itself spontaneously by means of its class will or social will.

The state, then, did not exist from all eternity. There have been societies without it, that had no idea of any state or public power. At a certain stage of economic development, which was of necessity accompanied by a division of society into classes, the state became the inevitable result of this division. We are now rapidly approaching a stage of evolution in production, in which the existence of classes has not only ceased to be a necessity, but becomes a positive fetter on production. Hence these classes must fall as inevitably as they once arose. The state must irrevocably fall with them. The society that is to reorganize production on the basis of a free and equal association of the producers, will transfer the machinery of state where it will then belong: into the Museum of Antiquities by the side of the spinning wheel and the bronze ax. (*Origin of the Family*, pp. 211-212.)

When ultimately it [the state] becomes really representative of society as a whole, it makes itself superfluous. As soon as there is no longer any class of society to be held in subjection; as soon as, along with class domination and the struggle for individual existence based on the former anarchy of production, the collisions and excesses arising from these have also been abolished, there is nothing more to be repressed which would make a special repressive force, a state, necessary. (*Anti-Duhring*, p. 315.)

At the very best it [the state] is an inheritance of evil, bound to be transmitted to the proletariat when it has become victorious in its struggle for class supremacy, and the worst features of which it will have to lop off at once . . . until a new race, grown up under new, free social conditions, will be in a position to shake off from itself this State rubbish in its entirety. (Engels, Introduction to the German edition of *The Civil War in France*, p. 381.)

Marx and Engels can dispense with the state and still await socialism," since the socialism that they have in mind has nothing to do with the state. It is not a state socialism they think of, but a socialism in which "society" itself carries out all the decisions of the class will. Engels can speak of the withering away of the state, since it is not the state, but "society" that is to seize the means of production and operate them in accord with a "social" plan.

The fatal flaw in the argument is the fact that the class will is a fiction. A collective mind or will of the sort envisioned by Marx and Engels is a psychological impossibility. A number of individuals may desire the same thing and think in similar fashion, but it is still several minds that are at work, not a single collective mind. The unity possessed by the object desired must not be attributed to the persons desiring it. The existence of a high degree of agreement among the members of a group on certain questions cannot be accepted as establishing complete unanimity on all questions. Furthermore, it is one thing to maintain that the members of society are in complete agreement on a goal to be attained and quite another to assume that without direction or organization of any kind they will act as one person in working toward that goal. There can be, in short, no socialism that is not state socialism.

The class will idea has only to be understood to be seen for the fiction it is. Why, then, did Marx and Engels accept a concept so out of touch with reality? The answer is suggested by the anarchic nature of the Marxian conception of freedom. This conception of freedom is implicit in virtually everything that Marx and Engels wrote but it stands out with particular clarity in passages that deal with the classless society.

> . . . while in communist society, where nobody has one exclusive sphere of activity but each can become accomplished in any branch he wishes, society regulates the general production and thus makes it possible for me to do one thing to-day and another to-morrow, to hunt in the morning, fish in the afternoon, rear cattle in the evening, criticize after dinner, just as I have a mind, without ever becoming hunter, fisherman, shepherd or critic. (*German Ideology*, p. 22.)

"Society" is to regulate the "general production," but the individual is to remain free "to hunt in the morning, fish in the afternoon, rear cattle in the evening," just as he has a mind. If society is to regulate production, then it would seem that the actions of every individual must in some way be curtailed and regulated. But apparently not. The regulation of production does not seem to entail the regulation of persons. Complete social coordination is to exist, yet each individual is to be entirely free from compulsion and regulation.

The Marxian conception of the freedom-authority problem is essentially that of the anarchist. To Marx and Engels, as to the anarchists, men were either free or they were unfree. Freedom they conceived as an unqualified thing. Men were free only when they were as anarchically free as the individual pictured in the passage quoted above. Marx and Engels never wrote of the necessity of limiting freedom in some areas in order to increase it in others. They sought not a limited freedom, but an absolute freedom.

Since they thought in terms of absolute freedom, authority and freedom necessarily appear as incompatible. When authority exists, freedom cannot. When freedom exists authority cannot. This view necessarily dooms the state. If men can never be free so long as they are coerced, and if the state is an instrument of coercion, then men can only become free when the state is abolished. The solution is clearly the anarchistic denial of the state. It is significant in this respect that while Marx and Engels quarreled with the anarchists, it was not the anarchist vision of a stateless, harmonious society of completely free individuals that they rejected, but the insistence that the state should be abolished overnight rather than be allowed to "wither away."

Once the Marxian conception of the freedom-authority problem is grasped, the function served by the class will notion becomes clear. Only this ingenious doctrine can make plausible the Marxian view that absolute social solidarity and absolute individual freedom are capable of coexisting within a society. The doctrine of the class will is used by Marx and

Engels to overcome the problem stated so succinctly by Rousseau:

> 'The problem is to find a form of association which will defend and protect with the whole common force the person and goods of each associate, and in which each, while uniting himself with all, may still obey himself alone, and remain as free as before.' (Rousseau, *Social Contract*, Everyman's Library, New York: E. P. Dutton and Co., 1946, p. 12.)

How can each unite himself with all and still obey only himself? This happy state of affairs can exist only if each individual wills precisely what all other members of society will. But how can this unanimity be created? "This is the fundamental problem of which the *Social Contract* provides the solution." (*Ibid.*)

> '*Each of us puts his person and all his power in common under the supreme direction of the general will, and, in our corporate capacity, we receive each member as an indivisible part of the whole.'*

> At once, in place of the individual personality of each contracting party, this act of association creates a moral and collective body, composed of as many members as the assembly contains voters, and receiving from this act its unity, its common identity, its life, and its will. This public person, so formed by the union of all other persons, formerly took the name of *city*, and now takes that of *Republic* or *body politic.* . . . (*Ibid.*, p. 13.)

The act of association represented by the social contract creates, according to Rousseau, a "moral and collective body" in place of the various individual wills. By creating a "general will" identical with each individual's real will, it brings about the unanimity and complete merging of wills that is the indispensable prerequisite of a society in which absolute solidarity and absolute freedom can coexist. Since Rousseau poses the freedom-authority problem in terms of absolutes he can find no real solution for it but must "solve" it by means of a fiction such as the "general will." Marx, having posed it in the same fashion, has no recourse but to solve it by a similar device, the "class will."

The class will notion is less obviously preposterous than the general will idea because it is not thought to be created by a single act of association but, instead, is assumed to come into existence as the class itself is created.

> Along with the constantly diminishing number of the magnates of capital . . . grows the mass of misery, oppression, slavery, degradation, exploitation; but with this too grows the revolt of the working-class, a class always increasing in numbers, and disciplined, united, organized by the very mechanism of the process of capitalist production itself. (*Capital*, Vol. I, pp. 836-37.)

It has been shown that Marx and Engels assume the existence of a class will similar to Rousseau's general will, but it has not yet been shown how they attempt to establish the other points necessary for a Rousseauian solution of the problem. What, in the Marxian scheme, corresponds to Rousseau's tacit distinction between an individual's "real will" and his merely actual will? How, further, do Marx and Engels establish the identity of the class will with these individual "real wills"?

The answers to both these questions are suggested in the following passages by the peculiar way in which the term "instinct" is used:

> The great mass of the Blanquists at that time were socialists only because of their revolutionary proletarian instincts . . . (Engels, Introduction to *The Civil War in France*, p. 377.)

> These craftsmen, to their eternal honour, instinctively foresaw the future development of their class, and, though not fully conscious of the fact, were pressing forward toward organising themselves as the party of

[29]

the proletariat. (Engels, *History of the Communist League*, New York: International Publishers, 1933, p. 125.)

Whatever portion of the working class had become convinced of the insufficiency of mere political revolutions, and had proclaimed the necessity of a total social change, that portion, then called itself Communist. It was a crude, rough-hewn, purely instinctive sort of Communism; still, it touched the cardinal point . . . (Engels, Preface to the *Communist Manifesto*, p. 318.)

It is this notion of a "proletarian instinct," a deep, compelling, instinctive consciousness of class, that is the Marxian equivalent of the real will. The class-conscious individual is the individual who has perceived in a "crude, rough-hewn, purely instinctive" sort of way where his real interests lie. His "proletarian instinct" has allowed him to distinguish his real from his merely apparent interests. The idea of "real" *interests* is used more frequently than the idea of "real" *wills*, but the difference is insignificant since it is assumed that every individual "wills" as his interests dictate. Thus the second point is established.

All that the theory requires to be complete is the identification of the interests of the individual proletarian with the interests and will of his class. It is, of course, precisely this identification that Marx and Engels make when they state that what the individual proletarian perceives by means of his "proletarian instinct" is the importance of "class." The class-conscious individual perceives that *his real interests are class interests*. He perceives that his real interests are the same as those of every other proletarian, that they are one with those of his class.

It was shown in an earlier chapter that Marx and Engels habitually mistake the propositions and concepts of their theory for reality. That confusion is seen here quite clearly. The mystical awareness of class of which they write is possessed not by actual working men but by Marx's creations, his proto-type class members, his "proletarians." So with the class will. Marx and Engels write as if actual working men, taken as a group, possess this will, whereas only the ideal class of Marxian theory possesses it.

Since it is by means of the "real will" and "general will" doctrines that Marx and Engels seek to solve the freedom-authority problem, the fact that neither of these wills exist means that the problem is evaded rather than solved. Real and important problems of government are defined out of existence rather than dealt with.

The class-conscious individual is supposed to perceive the identity of his interests with those of his "class." Since, how-ever, there exists no proletarian instinct and no "class," as Marx and Engels use the term, there need exist no identity of interest between individual and "class."

The state is treated as unnecessary because of the assumed existence of the class will. Yet the class will does not exist. What organization, then, is to fill the vacuum created by the denial of the state and the non-existence of its supposed sub-stitute, the class will?

What should be the result when millions of people accept these Marxian fictions as realities? What will happen when these doctrines become the theoretical basis for a political movement? It is to the exploration of these questions that the bulk of Part II of this study will be devoted.

Before turning to this subject, however, it would seem de-sirable to inquire if there may not be some general explana-tion for what has appeared to be the most outstanding feature of the Marxian system of thought—the degree of its diver-gence from reality.

Chapter IV

Empiricism, A Priorism and the Marxian System

THE Marxian system represents a strange mixture of splendid insight on the one hand and astounding oversimplification and falsification of reality on the other. This peculiarity is not to be explained by ignorance, since Marx and Engels were learned men in a variety of fields. Nor is it to be explained by a failure to use empirical data. It is only necessary to read *Capital* in order to appreciate the enormous amount of material that must have been examined in the course of its writing. The explanation lies rather in the way in which the empirical elements in the thought of Marx and Engels were joined with the *a priori*.

Both men were empiricists operating within an *a priori* framework. The divergence of Marxist theory from reality can be understood only if it is realised that it was formula rather than fact, speculation rather than investigation, that determined its major outlines. This is not to say that Marx and Engels thought unfailingly in an *a priori* fashion, but rather that their key propositions owe more to their philosophical presuppositions than to their researches.

Neither man made a secret of the debt he owed to Hegel. In the preface to the second edition of *Capital* Marx states that he openly avowed himself "the pupil of that mighty thinker." In *Ludwig Feuerbach* Engels speaks of the dialectic as "our best working tool and our sharpest weapon." (*Ludwig Feuerbach*, p. 384.) "Hegel was not simply put aside," Engels states at another point in that work. "On the contrary, one started out from his revolutionary side . . . from the dialectical method." (*Ibid.*, p. 383.)

Marx and Engels did indeed "start out" from Hegel. In their early joint works, *The Holy Family* and *The German Ideology*, the Hegelian influence is apparent on almost every page. In these works, in which the outlines of the Marxian system were first set down, many of the ideas of Marx and Engels can be seen being derived from the Hegelian scheme. Both the language and the mode of thought are Hegelian.

Proletariat and wealth are antitheses. As such they constitute a whole; both are manifestations of the world of private property. . . . Private property as private property, as wealth, is compelled to preserve its own existence, and along with it that of its antithesis, the proletariat. Private property satisfied in itself is the positive side of the antithesis. The proletariat, on the other hand, is obliged, as proletariat, to abolish itself, and along with it private property, its conditioned antithesis, which makes it the proletariat . . .

Within the antithesis, therefore, the owner of private property is the conservative, and the proletarian is the destructive party. From the former proceeds the action of maintaining the antithesis, from the latter the action of destroying it. From the point of view of its national, economic development, private property is, of course, continually being driven towards its own dissolution, but only by an unconscious development which is independent of it, and which exists against its will, and is limited by the nature of things; only, that is, by creating the proletariat as proletariat, poverty conscious of its own physical and spiritual poverty, and demoralized humanity conscious of its own demoralization and consequently striving against it.

The proletariat fulfils the judgment which private property by the creation of the proletariat suspends over itself, just as it fulfils the judgment which wage-labour suspends over itself in creating alien riches and its own condemnation. If the proletariat triumphs, it does not thereby become the absolute side of society, for it triumphs only by abolishing itself and its opposite. In this way both the proletariat and its conditioned opposite, private property, are done away with. (Marx, *The Holy Family*, reprinted in part in *Selected Essays*, trans. H. J. Stenning. London: Leonard Parsons, 1926, pp. 177-79.)

When *The German Ideology* was completed in 1846, the Marxian scheme had been worked out in all its essential aspects. The significant point is that this work was completed *before* Marx began his serious study of political economy and history and long before he undertook the extensive research that preceded his publication of Volume I of *Capital*. The apparatus of empirical investigation was used by Marx and Engels not to suggest new hypotheses but to support conclusions which they had long since reached.

It goes without saying that my recapitulation of mathematics and the natural sciences was undertaken in order to convince myself in detail—of what in general I was not in doubt—that amid the welter of innumerable changes taking place in nature, the same dialectical laws of motion are in operation as those which in history govern the apparent fortuitousness of events . . . (Engels, Second Preface to *Anti-Duhring*, p. 16.)

It is noteworthy that Marx never found it necessary to alter in an important fashion any of the major propositions that he and Engels first propounded when they were young men.

In the accounts that they have given of the origin of "dialectical materialism," Marx and Engels make quite clear their *a priori* and rather mechanical mode of operation. They were both Hegelians at first. They participated in the "triumphal procession" (*Ludwig Feuerbach*, p. 362) of the Hegelian philosophy. With the publication of Feuerbach's *Essence of Christianity*, however, they were converted from Hegel's idealism to Feuerbach's materialism.

Then came Feuerbach's *Essence of Christianity.* With one blow it pulverized the contradiction, in that without circumlocutions it placed materialism on the throne again. . . . Nothing exists outside nature and man, and the higher beings our religious phantasies have created are only the fantastic reflection of our own essence. The spell was broken; the "system" was exploded and cast aside, and the contradiction, shown to exist only in our imagination, was dissolved. One must himself have experienced the liberating effect of this book to get an idea of it. Enthusiasm was general; we all became at once Feuerbachians. How enthusiastically Marx greeted the new conception and how much—in spite of all critical reservations—he was influenced by it, one may read in *The Holy Family.* (Engels, *Ludwig Feuerbach*, p. 364.)

But "Hegel was not simply put aside." (*Ibid.*, p. 383.) His dialectic was retained, and to it was engrafted materialism.

According to Hegel, therefore, the dialectical development apparent in nature and history, i.e., the causal interconnection of the progressive movement from the lower to the higher . . . is only a miserable copy of the self-movement of the concept going on from eternity, no one knows where, but at all events independently of any thinking human brain. This ideological reversal had to be done away with. We comprehended the concepts in our heads once more materialistically—as images of real things instead of regarding real things as images of this or that stage of development of the absolute concept. . . . Thereby the dialectic of the concept itself became merely the conscious reflex of the dialectical motion of the real world and thus the dialectic of Hegel was placed upon its head; or rather, turned off its head, on which it was standing before, and placed upon its feet. (*Ibid.*, p. 384.)

Thus, by joining the dialectic and materialism, "dialectical materialism" was produced. Marx and Engels believed that they had synthesized the best element in French thought, materialism, with the greatest achievement of German thought, the Hegelian dialectic. The operation was neat, having but one fault. When materialism is joined with the idea of dialectical development a logical monstrosity is created. The two elements can be placed side by side, as they have been in "dialectical materialism," but they are incapable of being joined in any meaningful fashion.

It is one thing to imagine logical concepts contradicting and negating one another, but how can "matter" be "negated"? And how is one to conceive of the negation of the negation when it is "matter" that is involved? In an effort to overcome the difficulties created by the juxtaposition of two such disparate ideas as the dialectic and materialism, Engels resorts to forced constructions like the following. He treats such things as germination, death, and the shattering of rock formations as "negations."

Let us take a grain of barley. Millions of such grains of barley are milled, boiled and brewed and then consumed. But if such a grain of barley meets with conditions which for it are normal, if it falls on suitable soil, then under the influence of heat and moisture a specific change takes place, it germinates; the grain as such ceases to exist, it is negated, and in its place appears the plant which has arisen from it, the negation of the grain. But what is the normal life-process of this plant? It grows, flowers, is fertilised and finally once more produces grains of barley, and as soon as these have ripened the stalk dies, is in its turn negated. As a result of this negation of the negation we have . . . (*Anti-Duhring*, p. 154.)

Butterflies, for example, spring from the egg through a negation of the egg, they pass through certain transformations until they reach sexual maturity, they pair and are in turn negated, dying as soon as the pairing process has been completed and the female has laid its numerous eggs. (*Ibid.*)

Furthermore, the whole of geology is a series of negated negations, a series arising from the successive shattering of old and the depositing of new rock formations. (*Ibid.*, p. 155.)

Characteristics of the Marxian scheme that cannot otherwise be accounted for become quite understandable once it is realized that the scheme is primarily an *a priori* construction. From Hegel Marx learned to impute a single great law of development to the universe and to everything in it. Here is, of course, the source of Marx's fusion of nature and history. They are treated as essentially identical since both are thought to unfold according to the same dialectical laws. From Hegel also Marx and Engels probably learned that fallacious mode of thinking which treats a demonstration of change, a demonstration of flux, as a demonstration of progress and development.

> This newer German philosophy culminated in the Hegelian system, in which for the first time—and this is its great merit—the whole natural, historical and spiritual world was presented as a process, that is, as in constant motion, change, transformation and development . . . (*Anti-Duhring*, p. 30.)

Having moved from the fact of change to the presumption of progress or development, it remained for Marx to say what it was that history was progressing toward. What is the "higher form to which present society is irresistibly tending"? (*Civil War in France*, p. 408.) All successive historical conditions "are only transitory stages in the endless course of development of human society from the lower to the higher," said Engels (*Ludwig Feuerbach*, p. 359), but what is the goal? While Hegel saw history as unfolding "dialectically" toward its climax in the Prussian state of his own day, Marx envisioned it as reaching its climax in the future achievement of what he called a "classless society."

Marx had learned that the dialectic provides a splendid means for attributing one's own values to the historical process. It allows an individual to impute his own desires to history in the guise of having learned "History's" laws. Marx attacked Saint-Simon, Fourier and Owen, the "utopian socialists" as he called them, because, he said, they were trying to achieve their desires in the face of a universe indifferent to those desires. It was unfortunate, he implied, that they could not have studied history and learned the laws of its development, learned, that is, that all nature develops dialectically, that all history is the history of class struggles, that a revolution will come to pass in which a "class" called the bourgeoisie will be overcome by another "class" called the proletariat and that the victory of the latter will lead to the advent of the classless society.

Of these two views it is not difficult to perceive which is the more truly utopian. The "utopian socialists" acknowledged their values to be values, admitted their likes and dislikes and strove to bring about the perfect society they desired. The hard-headed "scientific socialist" Marx, on the other hand, preferred to attribute his personal values to history, to assume that "History" would bring to pass of its own accord the things he desired.

There is an important utopian element in the thinking of the "utopian socialists," however, and it is interesting to note that Marx and Engels never perceived it. Saint-Simon, Fourier and Owen viewed human nature as wholly the product of the social environment and, consequently, as infinitely malleable and infinitely perfectible. Since they shared this view, Marx and Engels completely failed to perceive its utopian nature.

Marx may well have been predisposed to a single-factor theory of history by his early training in the Hegelian system. The economic factor plays a role in the Marxian scheme equivalent to that played in Hegel's system by the "spirit."

According to Hegel all historical developments are to be explained in terms of what he called the Spirit. With Marx, however, it is not the Spirit but the economic factor which alone is operative in history and which one-sidedly causes all things. That Marx should have hit upon the economic factor as his single cause is not, so far as can be seen, to be attributed to the Hegelian influence. What is to be attributed to the Hegelian influence, however, is the way in which he conceived this factor to operate once he had selected it.

By the same token, Marx's use of the concept of "class" is not to be explained wholly in terms of Hegel's influence. The dialectic can have exerted only a negative influence in this case. It merely established the specifications that any concept Marx used would have to satisfy, were it caste, class, race, nation or something else. The dialectic required only that the entities used in connection with it be few in number, that they appear capable of conflicting, that they be easily thought of as coming into existence, developing, and passing away, and that they be easily reduced in number when it became necessary for a dialectical conflict to appear clear-cut. Marx's selection of the idea of "class" from the number of concepts that would have satisfied these requirements must be explained in terms of the great gap that existed between rich and poor when he wrote, and the prominent role that the conception of class was playing in French historical writing at the time.

Once he had selected the concept of class and inserted it into the Hegelian scheme, certain other features of the Marxian view of history follow naturally. His "classes" were viewed as representing logical extremes, oppressors and oppressed, exploiters and enslaved, because they had to represent the "thesis" and "antithesis" of an Hegelian triad. They had to be "contradictions" equivalent to Hegel's Being and Nothing. They had to conflict for a similar reason. In a dialectical universe all contradictions must conflict.

Marx's fictitious class members, his proletarians and his

bourgeois, are to be explained in a similar fashion. They were created to inhabit his classes. Since Marx's classes were supposed to be composed of millions of totally enslaved persons on the one hand, and millions of callous exploiters on the other, such persons had to be assumed to exist. Having created a world of his own, he needed to create people to live in it.*

Hegel saw every aspect of a culture, its philosophy, art, law, politics and so on, as a manifestation of the Spirit. The Marxian equivalents of this view are the notions of "ideology" and "superstructure;" the belief that the thought and institutions of an epoch are reflections of the existing stage in the development of the means of production. Marx needed only to insert the economic factor in place of Hegel's Spirit and these famous Marxian concepts were complete.

If history is to be regarded as developing according to immutable laws such as Marx portrayed, then a psychology must be attributed to men that allows them no freedom to disobey those laws. Marx and Engels assumed that humans are the wholly passive reflectors of their environment. Without this assumption they would not have been free to ignore human beings while concentrating on the conflicts and contradictions of their great abstractions.

In the Marxian scheme the sociological doctrines, class, class struggle, the importance of the economic factor and so on, are treated as given, and the psychological and other as-

---

*The state of mind in which Marx elaborated this scheme might have been similar to that described by Rousseau in the following passage from his *Confessions*:

The impossibility of grasping realities threw me into the land of chimeras, and, seeing nothing in existence which was worthy of my enthusiasm, I sought nourishment for it in an ideal world, which my fertile imagination soon peopled with beings after my own heart.... In my continued ecstasies, I intoxicated myself with full draughts of the most delightful sensations that have ever entered the heart of man. I entirely forgot the human race, and created for myself societies of perfect beings, heavenly alike in their beauties and virtues; trusty, tender, and loyal friends such as I never found in this world below. (Rousseau, *Confessions*, New York: The Modern Library, n.d., pp. 441-42.)

sumptions necessary to make them plausible are simply taken for granted. In order to appear valid, the Marxian sociology required the existence of some mechanism by means of which economic facts could determine the thoughts and actions of men. Since no such mechanism existed, Marx had the choice of modifying his sociology or falsifying human psychology. The sociological doctrines were retained and the necessary psychological assumptions were made without hesitation.

Marx's views on the ineffectiveness of political action follow from his conviction that the relations of production constitute the economic substructure of society and his belief that "classes" must necessarily war to the death. Since political power is but a reflection of economic power and since the bourgeoisie is the dominant economic class, it follows that it must necessarily be the dominant political power, that is, it must control the state apparatus. Since, further, the bourgeoisie and the proletariat are engaged in a life and death struggle, the proletariat cannot hope to accomplish anything by acting through the bourgeois parliament. Hence the Marxian dogma that working people will never be able to better themselves in any significant fashion by parliamentary means.

As in Hegel's scheme the state is its own end, so in Marx's the class is its own end. Both are set above moral criticism. Marx's classes, like Hegel's states, are joined by no common bonds and owe no duties to one another. Between them only warfare can exist. And, further, as Hegel embodies the individual's real will in the state, so Marx embodies it in the "class."

It is now clear why the Marxian system was so fully elaborated when it first appeared. Great portions of it were fashioned by a more or less mechanical adaptation of a number of Hegelian ideas, and still other parts of it were constructed to fit in with the ideas so adapted. The wonder is not that the scheme is so out of accord with reality, but that it is not more so.

On the other hand, many of the merits as well as many of the faults of various Marxian ideas are to be explained by the fact that the system was constructed, so to speak, from the top down. By adopting many of Hegel's ideas and altering them according to his own predilections, Marx emerged with something which was in many respects original and suggestive. The same cast of mind that allowed Marx to elaborate a scheme with so little regard for reality allowed him, at the same time, to escape the influence of many of the dogmas of his time. While the world that Marx created was a caricature of the real world, that caricature did, by its very oversimplification, emphasize certain aspects of the real world.

Many conceptions that are commonplace today were either created or popularized by Marx and Engels. Their writings have brought home to countless people the importance of economic factors to an understanding of history and contemporary society. They pointed out many of the problems created by an unregulated capitalism and focused attention on the difficulties growing out of the development of modern industry and the formation of an urban working population, an urban proletariat in the non-Marxian sense of that term. The concepts of "ideology" and "superstructure" are today familiar tools of analysis largely thanks to Marx and Engels. In reviving a concept of class, they opened a great new area to social and historical investigation and in their conception of human nature they suggested a radically new starting point for thinking about man and society.

Each insight, however, is so overlaid with distortion and oversimplification that it is frequently difficult to separate the useful from the useless. The reflection psychology and the doctrine of ideology are such oversimplifications. The Marxian world is peopled with automatons who have no characteristic other than that of reflecting their class, and thus their own, economic interests. Because there is but one explanation of human nature consistent with these presuppositions, Marx and Engels are incapable of dealing with ideas or behavior that run counter to economic interests or are irrelevant to them. An enormous range of human behavior is thus closed to their understanding.

The same oversimplification is to be found in the Marxian treatment of the problems of an industrial society. Marx and Engels perceived the monotony of specialized industrial work and the atomizing effect that it has on human personalities. They saw the hierarchy and discipline that are a part of large-scale industry and they perceived the way in which individuals are submerged in giant industrial concerns. They saw these things, and the indictment they drew up against them was powerful.

The indictment proved effective as a club against the old society, but it offered little in the way of a positive program. What does the Marxian scheme suggest as a remedy for the ill effects of specialization? What are Marx's recommendations for dealing with the problems of hierarchy and discipline in industry? The answer is that the writings of Marx and Engels contain no real program for remedying the defects of bourgeois society. Their proletarian revolution serves as a focal point for emotion and agitation without providing solutions of a practical nature to the real problems that exist.

By virtue of his failure to distinguish the industrial process from "capitalism" Marx was able to assume that all the evils which he depicted would be swept out of existence when "capitalism" itself ceased to exist. He failed to distinguish those evils which were inherent in the industrial process from those which were not. Instead of offering concrete proposals and alternative arrangements, Marx and Engels were satisfied to state the problem in such a fashion that, by definition, those evils could not exist in their future society.

Marx and Engels dismissed carelessness, greed, desire for power and even sheer, gratuitous evil in the same way they dismissed the problems of large-scale industry. All elements in human nature that they found undesirable or ignoble they declared to be the products of a "class society." Since these characteristics were the result of class society, they were certain to vanish when the classes themselves vanished. Are men covetous? Covetousness is the product of a class society, and will vanish with the disappearance of classes.

Because of its determinist and environmentalist premises, the Marxian system is devoid of any genuine concept of evil. All that is bad in the world is explained in terms of bad institutions which have somehow come into existence. Once these have been done away with, misery will become a thing of the past. A revolution is to come to pass in which the oppressed are to take over the rule of society. After this single apocalyptic event all the problems that have troubled "bourgeois" society will automatically be resolved. As people become used to observing the fundamental decencies of life the perfect classless society will be ushered in, and good will have triumphed over evil once and for all.

The Marxist view of man's destiny and his place in the world appears as shallow and immature as it does largely because of this oversimplification. The advent of a perfect society and the solution of all the problems that have vexed mankind from the beginning is momentarily expected. Marx and Engels never understood that men will always have serious problems to deal with, and that while some may be solved, others will remain and new ones will arise to take the place of those that have been solved. There is lacking any "tragic sense of life," any sense of life's inevitable difficulty. One is inclined to observe with Hamlet:

There are more things in heaven and earth, Horatio,
Than are dreamt of in your philosophy.

Marxism provides its adherents with what might be called a get-rich-quick philosophy. Men do not need to work toward the ends they desire in order to achieve those ends. Men do not have to practice cooperation in order to achieve a completely cooperative society, nor to eschew violence in order to arrive at a world without violence. "History" is to bring all these things to pass.

Along with everything else, human history is oversimplified. "The history of all hitherto existing society is the history of class struggles." History is thus reduced to the working out of a single factor, the economic, and to a single oft-repeated pattern, that of class struggle. Instead of being the result of a baffling interplay of numerous factors, it becomes very simple indeed. No effort need be exerted to discover the complex motives that impelled men in a given historical situation. It is known beforehand that all persons act as they do because they reflect the position of their class.

Just as the past is an open book to Marx, so is the future. The same "laws" and "tendencies" that were found to hold in the past are simply projected into the future. In projecting these "tendencies," Marx and Engels make no allowance for the development of tendencies running counter to those they depict. The proletariat is to be exploited until the question becomes a simple one of revolution or extinction. They appear almost never to have considered the possibility that remedial action might be taken to counter the developments which they portrayed, that social legislation with regard to wages, hours and working conditions might prove effective, and that the power to tax might be used to reduce gross inequalities of income and to establish social security systems.

This study has, thus far, concerned itself primarily with Marxist theory and the extent to which that theory is out of accord with reality. From this point on the focus will be altered. The stage has now been set, and it is time to let our knowledge of Marxist theory illuminate the subject of modern Communism as best it may.

PART II

CHAPTER V

Theory and Practice: I

WHAT is the relation of Marxist and Marxist-Leninist theory to Communist practice? On no point dealt with by writers on Communism and the Soviet Union is confusion more deep and more general than on this seemingly simple question. It will be the aim of this chapter to disperse that confusion.

Briefly, "theory" will be shown to follow rather than to precede practice. It will be shown that the Dictator can do as he will with Marxist and Marxist-Leninist theory since he is its interpreter-creator. In this chapter the role of the Dictator as the manufacturer of theory will be demonstrated, first in connection with the question of compromise, and second in connection with the famous Marxian doctrine of the "withering away" of the state.

Taken together, the writings of Marx and Engels amount to many thousands of pages. Yet of this great mass of material not more than ten or fifteen pages are devoted to a treatment of what is to follow the proletarian revolution. In *Capital*, his three volume attempt to depict the inner laws of capitalist development, Marx seldom refers to the classless society, and the phrase "dictatorship of the proletariat" is nowhere used. Marx and Engels were primarily critics of the existing order. They were far more interested in pointing out the shortcomings of that order than they were in considering the problems that would have to be dealt with after the occurrence of the "proletarian revolution." The criticisms they leveled at the society of their time are detailed and powerful, but when they come to speak of the period that is to follow the revolution they speak in terms of the greatest generality.

This neglect of the many practical problems that must follow a successful revolution, particularly a revolution as thoroughgoing as the one envisioned by Marx and Engels, is easily understood in terms of the determinist element in the Marxian scheme. Marx believed that the same inevitable development that was to sweep capitalist society away would create a perfectly functioning proletarian society. Since "History" was going to take care of this matter, it was not necessary that he agitate himself about the precise forms and institutions which would have to be developed to provide for "the administration of things and the direction of the process of production." Interest in all such practical problems was dubbed "utopian." Lenin has presented this view a number of times.

> Marx did not drop into utopia; he expected the *experience* of the mass movement to provide the reply to the question of the exact forms the organization of the proletariat as the ruling class will assume and the exact manner in which this organisation will be combined with the most complete, most consistent "winning of the battle of democracy." (Lenin, *The State and Revolution*, reprinted in *Essentials of Lenin*, London: Lawrence and Wishart, 1947, Vol. II, p. 168.)
> There is no trace of an attempt on Marx's part to conjure up a utopia, to make idle guesses about what cannot be known. (*Ibid.*, p. 198.)

It is, however, to precisely these writings that Lenin claims to turn for guidance in dealing with complex post-revolutionary problems. They are treated as a storehouse of practical advice on matters such as agricultural policy and industrial production even though they touch on the problems of a post-revolutionary society only slightly and were written, many of them, half a century before the October Revolution. The belief that these few pages provide detailed advice on a multitude of contemporary problems can only be viewed as a superstition or a myth. It is as if the passage in the American Constitution granting to Congress the right to "regulate commerce with foreign nations and among the several states..." were looked to for guidance in connection with technical difficulties involved in radio communications or air transport regulation.

If the official conception of the relation of theory to practice must be rejected as preposterous, there still remains the problem of understanding the actual relationship. This understanding can best be advanced by a study of several examples of the way in which theory has been used by Lenin and Stalin. Here, for instance, are some of Lenin's passages on the subject of compromise.

> The conclusion to be drawn is clear: to reject compromises "on principle," to reject the admissibility of compromises in general, no matter of what kind, is childishness, which is difficult even to take seriously.
> (*Essentials of Lenin*, Vol. II, p. 584.)

It is absurd, Lenin says, to be against compromises in general. Each compromise should, instead, be judged on its own merits.

> The strictest loyalty to the ideas of Communism must be combined with the ability to make all the necessary practical compromises, to manoeuvre, to make agreements, zigzags, retreats and so on ... (*Ibid.*, p. 628.)

> There are compromises and compromises. One must be able to analyse the situation and the concrete conditions of each compromise, or of each variety of compromise. (*Ibid.*, p. 584.)

> It is important to single out from the practical questions of the politics of each separate or specific historical moment those which reveal the principal type of impermissible, treacherous compromises, compromises embodying the opportunism that is fatal to the revolu-

tionary class, and to exert all efforts to explain them and combat them. (*Ibid.*, p. 608.)

Who is to decide, however, whether a given compromise is of the necessary or the treacherous variety?

A political leader who desires to be useful to the revolutionary proletariat must know how to single out *concrete* cases when such compromises are inadmissible, as expressive of opportunism and *treachery*, and direct all the force of criticism, the full edge of merciless exposure and relentless war, against *those* *concrete* compromises . . . (*Ibid.*, p. 584.)

A "political leader" decides which are the permissible and which the inadmissible compromises. Against those which are, in his opinion, inadmissible, he must direct "all the force of criticism, the full edge of merciless exposure and relentless war." There is no doubt that the "political leader" Lenin has in mind is himself, since he proceeds to make exactly the sort of decision he has just described.

In the same year, 1918, the most prominent representatives of "Left Communism," for example, Radek and Bukharin, openly admitted their mistake. It had seemed to them that the Brest-Litovsk Peace was a compromise with the imperialists that was inadmissible on principle and harmful to the party of the revolutionary proletariat. It really was a compromise with the imperialists, but it was a compromise which, under the circumstances, was *obligatory*. (*Ibid.*, p. 583.)

It is Lenin who is to analyse each situation and decide whether compromise would represent flexibility or treachery. If he decides to compromise, then that compromise, automatically, becomes one of the "necessary" or "obligatory" compromises and stands as a testimonial to the flexibility of his leadership. If he decides not to compromise, the projected compromise automatically becomes a treacherous abandonment of the interests of the proletariat. Once Lenin has made his decision, those of a different persuasion are ipso facto mistaken.

The absence of a detailed treatment of post-revolutionary problems in the writings of Marx and Engels was, on the whole, an aid to Lenin. It meant that he was occasionally handicapped when he sought to justify his actions by citing their writings but it meant also that he was rarely embarrassed by statements and prophecies made by Marx and Engels. Had those two been more concerned with the difficulties to be encountered in a post-revolutionary society there would certainly have been more forecasts like that of the "withering away" of the state for Lenin and Stalin to explain. The problem of the state is a vexed one in the writings of Lenin and Stalin and provides, for that reason, a particularly fertile field in which the study of the relation between theory and practice may be carried on.

In its outline form the problem is easily understood. Marx and Engels, believing as they did in the existence of the class will, felt free to forecast the "withering away" of the state after the revolution. Since there is no class will, however, and since every society requires an organizing or directing agency of some kind, the state has shown no sign of withering away. The problem is thus one of reconciling an allegedly scientific Marxist prediction with the reality of a state apparatus of ever-increasing strength.

Only after the seizure of power did the issue appear in this clear-cut form. Until that time, Lenin was still free to write primarily in terms of the class will strain of Marxist thought. In *State and Revolution*, written shortly before the October Revolution, passages like the following are found.

> We set ourselves the ultimate aim of abolishing the state, *i.e.*, all organized and systematic violence, all use of violence against men in general. . . . But in striving for Socialism we are convinced that it will develop into Communism, and, hence that the need for violence against people in general, the need for the

subjection of one man to another, and of one section of the population to another, will vanish, since people will *become accustomed* to observing the elementary conditions of social life *without force* and *without subordination.* (*Essentials of Lenin*, Vol. II, p. 197.)

Only in Communist Society, when the resistance of the capitalists has been completely broken, when the capitalists have disappeared, when there are no classes . . . *only* then does "the state . . . cease to exist," and it *"becomes possible to speak of freedom."* Only then will really complete democracy, democracy without any exceptions, be possible . . . owing to the simple fact that, freed from capitalist slavery, from the untold horrors, savagery, absurdities and infamies of capitalist exploitation, people will gradually *become accustomed* to observing the elementary rules of social intercourse . . . they will become accustomed to observing them without force, without compulsion, without subordination, *without the special apparatus* for compulsion which is called the state. (*Ibid.*, pp. 201-202.)

Only now can we appreciate to the full the correctness of Engels' remarks in which he mercilessly ridiculed the absurdity of combining the words "freedom" and "state." While the state exists there is no freedom. When there will be freedom, there will be no state. (*Ibid.*, p. 206.)

Finally, only Communism makes the state absolutely unnecessary, for there is *nobody* to be suppressed —"nobody" in the sense of *a class*, in the sense of a systematic struggle against a definite section of the population. We are not utopians, and we do not in the least deny the possibility and inevitability of excesses on the part of *individual persons*, or the need to suppress *such* excesses. But, in the first place, no special machine, no special apparatus of repression is needed for this; this will be done by the armed people

itself, as simply and as readily as any crowd of civil-
ized people, even in modern society, parts two people
who are fighting, or interferes to prevent a woman
from being assaulted. (*Ibid.*, p. 203.)

Apparently aware of the utopian nature of this mode of
thought, Lenin overlooked no opportunity to insist that it was
not utopian. It was, he insisted, all very scientific.

And of course we are not losing ourselves in a
Utopia, we are not ceasing to look at things in a sober,
practical way . . . (Lenin, *Collected Works*, New
York: International Publishers, 1932, Vol. XXI. Bk.
2, p. 33.)

We are not Utopians. (*Ibid.*, p. 35.)

There is no trace of utopianism in Marx, in the
sense that he invented or imagined a "new" society.
No, he studied the *birth* of the new society *from* the
old, the forms of transition from the latter to the
former as a natural-historical process. (*Essentials of
Lenin*, Vol. II, p. 173.)

Marx treats the question of Communism in the same
way as a naturalist would treat the question of the
development, say, of a new biological species, if he
knew that such and such was its origin and such and
such the direction in which it was changing. (*Ibid.*, p.
198.)

Lenin himself, quite plainly, did not expect the state to
wither away immediately after the revolution, since along
with the class will strain in *State and Revolution* went many
warnings that this withering away had to be relegated to the
very distant future.

Clearly there can be no question of defining the
exact moment of the *future* "withering away"—the
more so since it must obviously be a rather lengthy
process. (*Ibid.*)

The essence of Marx's doctrine of the state is assimi-
lated only by those who understand that the dictator-

ship of a *single* class is necessary not only for class society in general, not only for the *proletariat* which has overthrown the bourgeoisie, but for the entire *historical period* which separates capitalism from "classless society," from Communism. (*Ibid.*, p. 164.)

While giving lip service to the class will strand of thought with its talk of the state's withering away, Lenin actually reintroduced through the back door the state which Marx and Engels had ejected through the front. *State and Revolution* might almost be regarded as written for this purpose. In it Lenin combats the withering away doctrine accepted at that time as the orthodox Marxian view. He sought to alter this view by emphasizing a distinction that played only a small part in the writings of Marx and Engels; the difference between the lower and higher phases of communism. The state is to wither away, said Lenin, *only* when the higher phase of communism is reached, an "entire historical period" from the time at which the proletariat seizes power. *Until* that time the "dictatorship of the proletariat" will exist and *with it the state*.

If this view appears to conflict with the suggestion of Engels' famous passage that the state withers away *immediately* after the revolution, Lenin need only insist that what Engels really meant was that while the *bourgeois* state is put an end to at once, the *proletarian* state withers away only much later.

In the first place, Engels at the very outset of his argument says that, in assuming state power, the proletariat by that "puts an end to the state as the state." It is not "good form" to ponder over what this means. ... As a matter of fact, Engels speaks here of "putting an end" to the *bourgeois* state by the proletarian revolution, while the words about its withering away refer to the remnants of the *proletarian* state after the Socialist revolution. According to Engels, the bourgeois state does not "wither away," but is *"put an end to"* by the proletariat in the course of the revolution. What withers away after the revolution is the proletarian state or semi-state. (*Ibid.*, pp. 151-152.)

Lenin seeks to escape the problem by casting the withering away of the state so far into the future that it ceases to be embarrassing. "For the complete withering away of the state complete Communism is necessary." (*Ibid.*, p. 206.)

Until 1930 Stalin handled the difficulty in the same way. In that year, however, he advanced the following explanation for the growing power of the state.

> It may be said that such a way of approaching the question is "contradictory." But is there not the same "contradiction" in our treatment of the question of the State? We are in favour of the state dying out, and at the same time we stand for the strengthening of the dictatorship of the proletariat, which represents the most powerful and mighty authority of all forms of State which have existed up to the present day. The highest possible development of the power of the State, with the object of preparing the conditions for the dying out of the State: that is the Marxist formula. Is it "contradictory?" Yes, it is "contradictory." But this contradiction is a living thing, and completely reflects Marxist dialectics. (Stalin, *Leninism*, New York: International Publishers, 1933, Vol. II, p. 402.)

Stalin is saved by the dialectic. Why is the state becoming so powerful? In preparation for its "dying out," of course. Does this appear contradictory? It must be remembered that the dialectic thrives on contradiction, on the idea that all things turn into their opposites.

This argument does not represent a fundamental doctrinal change. It was not until 1936 when Stalin decreed that antagonistic classes no longer existed in the Soviet Union that a real change was made. Since, according to orthodox Marxist theory, the state is to vanish when classes disappear, its continued existence required some explanation. In an effort to settle the matter once and for all Stalin developed a wholly new "theory"—that of capitalist encirclement.

It is sometimes asked: "We have abolished the exploiting classes; there are no longer any hostile classes in the country; there is nobody to suppress; hence there is no more need of the state; it must die away. Why then do we not help our socialist state to die away? Why do we not strive to put an end to it? Is it not time to throw out all this rubbish of the state?"

Or further: "The exploiting classes have already been abolished in our country; socialism has been built in the main; we are advancing towards communism. Now, the Marxist doctrine of the state says that there is to be no state under communism. Why then do we not help our socialist state to die away? Is it not time we relegated the state to the museum of antiquities?"

These questions show that those who ask them have conscientiously memorized certain propositions contained in the doctrine of Marx and Engels about the state. But they also show that these comrades have failed to understand the essential meaning of this doctrine; that they have failed to realise in what historical conditions the various propositions of this doctrine were elaborated; and, what is more, that they do not understand present-day international conditions, have overlooked the capitalist encirclement and the dangers it entails for the socialist country. These questions not only betray an underestimation of the capitalist encirclement, but also an underestimation of the role and significance of the bourgeois states and their organs, which send spies, assassins and wreckers into our country and are waiting for a favorable opportunity to attack it by armed force. (Stalin, *From Socialism to Communism in the Soviet Union*, New York: International Publishers, 1939, p. 49-50.)

Those who ask these embarrassing questions are taking

the writings of Marx and Engels at face value without first seeking Stalin's opinion of their "essential meaning." Stalin finds that Engels, when he spoke of the withering away of the state, had in mind conditions quite different from those currently existing. Engels is, consequently, very much of a back number on this question.

Consider, for example, the classical formulation of the theory of the development of the socialist state given by Engels: (Then follows the passage that ends with 'The government of persons is replaced by the administration of things and the direction of the process of production. The state is not "abolished," it *withers* away.')

Is this proposition of Engels correct?

Yes, it is correct, but only on one of two conditions: (1) *if* we study the socialist state only from the angle of the internal development of the country, abstracting ourselves in advance from the international situation; isolating, for the convenience of investigation, the country and the state from the international situation; or (2) *if* we assume that socialism is already victorious in all countries, or in the majority of countries . . .

Well, but what if socialism has been victorious only in one country, and if, in view of this, it is quite impossible to abstract oneself from the international conditions—what then? Engels' formula does not furnish an answer to this question. As a matter of fact, Engels did not set himself this question, and therefore could not have given an answer to it . . .

But it follows from this that Engels' general formula about the destiny of the socialist state in general cannot be extended to the partial and specific case of the victory of socialism in one country only, a country which is surrounded by a capitalist world, is subject to the menace of foreign military attack, cannot therefore abstract itself from the international situation, and must have at its disposal a well-trained army, well organized punitive organs, and a strong intelligence service—consequently, must have its own state, strong enough to defend the conquests of socialism from foreign attack. (*Ibid.*, pp. 52-53.)

As long as the Soviet Union continues to be surrounded by non-Communist nations the state, with all its trimmings, will continue to exist. The problem of its date of disappearance is again dismissed by being cast into the indefinite future.

As ultimate authorities on theoretical matters, Lenin and Stalin have been able to manufacture "theory" to suit their own purposes. Never, however, has this been acknowledged. Instead they claim only to be "advancing," "enriching" and "extending" Marxist theory.

Lenin always was and remained a loyal and consistent pupil of Marx and Engels, and wholly and entirely based himself on the principles of Marxism. But Lenin did not merely carry out the doctrines of Marx and Engels. He developed these doctrines further. What does that mean? It means that he developed the doctrines of Marx and Engels in accordance with the new conditions of development, with the new phase of capitalism, and with imperialism. This means that in developing further the doctrines of Marx in the new conditions of the class struggle, Lenin contributed to the general treasury of Marxism something new as compared with what was created by Marx and Engels and with what they could create in the pre-imperialist period of capitalism. Moreover, the contribution made by Lenin to Marxism is based wholly and entirely on the principles laid down by Marx and Engels. In that sense we speak of Leninism as Marxism of the epoch of imperialism and proletarian revolutions. (*Leninism*, Vol. II, p. 43.)

In the name of the "advancing" and "enriching" of Marxist

theory Lenin and Stalin have jettisoned those of Marx's formulations which do not suit their purposes, and have replaced them by other more satisfactory doctrines.

As a result of a study of the experience of the two Russian revolutions, Lenin, on the basis of the theory of Marxism, arrived at the conclusion that the best political form for the dictatorship of the proletariat was not a parliamentary democratic republic, but a republic of Soviets. Proceeding from this, Lenin, in April 1917, during the period of transition from the bourgeois to the Socialist revolution, issued the slogan of a republic of Soviets as the best political form for the dictatorship of the proletariat. The opportunists of all countries clung to the parliamentary republic and accused Lenin of departing from Marxism and destroying democracy. But it was Lenin, of course, who was the real Marxist who had mastered the theory of Marxism and not the opportunists, for Lenin was advancing the Marxist theory by enriching it with new experience, whereas the opportunists were dragging it back and transforming one of its propositions into a dogma. (*History of the Communist Party of the Soviet Union*, (Authorized Edition,) New York: International Publishers, 1939, p. 356.)

Lenin and Stalin are able to "enrich" Marxist theory because they are able to distinguish between "its letter and substance."

Mastering the Marxist-Leninist theory does not at all mean learning all its formulas and conclusions by heart and clinging to their every letter. To master the Marxist-Leninist theory we must first of all learn to distinguish between its letter and substance. (*Ibid.*, p. 355.)

Because they, and presumably they alone, are able to make this distinction, Lenin and Stalin feel no hesitation in replacing the "antiquated" propositions in the Marxian scheme.

Mastering the Marxist-Leninist theory means being able to enrich this theory with the new experience of the revolutionary movement, with new propositions and conclusions, it means being able *to develop it and advance it* without hesitating to replace—in accordance with the substance of the theory—such of its propositions as have become antiquated by new ones corresponding to the new historical situation. (*Ibid.*, p. 356.)

Indeed, to fail to have the "courage" to replace one of the antiquated propositions might well bring about catastrophe.

What would have happened to the Party, to our revolution, to Marxism, if Lenin had been overawed by the letter of Marxism and had not had the courage of theoretical conviction to discard one of the old conclusions of Marxism and to replace it by a new conclusion affirming that the victory of Socialism in one country, taken singly, was possible, a conclusion which corresponded to the new historical conditions? The Party would have groped in the dark, the proletarian revolution would have been deprived of leadership, and the Marxist theory would have begun to decay. The proletariat would have lost, and the enemies of the proletariat would have won. (*Ibid.*, p. 357.)

The interpreter of Marxist theory occupies the same position that Goering occupied when he boasted, "I decide who is Aryan." Never, however, have either Lenin or Stalin made any remark as crude as this. Whereas Goering acknowledged, indeed flaunted, the arbitrary nature of his decisions, Lenin and Stalin have carefully hidden the arbitrary nature of theirs behind the appearance of objectivity. The emphasis that both have put on their ability to think "dialectically" is an example of this effort to mask the nature of their decisions as to what is and what is not good Marxist theory.

Whoever has failed to understand this peculiarity and "contradictoriness" of our transitional times, whoever has failed to understand this dialectical character of the historical process, is lost to Marxism.

The unfortunate thing for our deviators is that they do not understand this and do not want to understand Marxist dialectics. (*Leninism*, Vol. II, p. 403.)

This bit of mystification allows the chief interpreter of theory to maintain that he has reached his conclusions because he has mastered the intricacies of "dialectical" thinking. By emphasizing their alleged ability to think "dialectically," Lenin and Stalin suggest that those who disagree with them would not do so if they, too, were able to think dialectically. This is properly termed mystification since there is no "dialectical" manner of thinking. It is no more than a fiction which Lenin and Stalin have put to good use. The dialectic corresponds to no reality, so that one triad, one selection of stages is as good as another. It is a game anyone can play.

The praise of their abilities as theoreticians which Lenin and Stalin have encouraged represents a further effort on their part to obscure the interested nature of their theorizing.

It may be said without fear of exaggeration that since the death of Engels the master theoretician Lenin, and after Lenin, Stalin and the other disciples of Lenin, have been the only Marxists who have advanced the Marxist theory and who have enriched it with new experience in the new conditions of the class struggle of the proletariat. (*History of the C.P.S.U.*, p. 358.)

This chapter has advanced a view of the relationship between Marxist theory and Communist practice which shows theory serving, not as a guide to practice, but as a justification for it. Since Lenin and Stalin have taken such pains to obscure this relationship, the question of their reasons for doing so naturally arises. What have they stood to gain by the propagation of a conception so different from the actual one? Chapter VI will show that they have had very good reasons indeed.

Chapter VI

Theory and Practice: II

MARXIST and Marxist-Leninist theory is, for all practical purposes, whatever the Dictator says it is. The "unity of theory and practice" of which Lenin and Stalin have made so much is nothing more than a technique by means of which all decisions are justified, after the fact, in terms of theory. There are points of Marxist doctrine which Lenin and Stalin have not altered, but these have either already suited their purposes or have been so abstract as to be irrelevant to practical matters.

Lenin and Stalin achieved their positions as final authorities on Marxist theory not because of their ability as theoreticians, but because each was the most powerful figure in the Communist Party. Power, not reasoning ability or knowledge of Marxist writings, is the final arbiter on all points of theory. The Party boss has the final word since he is the only person who can force his views on all others. Power is never openly treated as decisive, however, since the usefulness of Marxist-Leninist theory as a means of control would be greatly diminished if the nature of its interpretation were widely understood.

Here then is the answer to the query of the preceding chapter. What function does their theorizing serve, that Lenin and Stalin should take such pains to disguise its subjective and interested nature? "Theory" is a potent instrument for the control of persons both within the Communist Party and without. Theorizing is never indulged in for its own sake. Behind every example there is a practical purpose. In the following passages, for example, Stalin is presumably merely "clearing up points of theory," merely pointing out what any student of Marxist thought might have perceived for himself, were he a sufficiently able theoretician. Yet it is important to note the practical purpose underlying these expositions of theory. Stalin undertakes to destroy the "equilibrium theory," the theory used to justify the continued existence of individual peasant farming, and in so doing strikes an important blow at that type of farming itself.

The new methods of actual practice are calling into being new methods of dealing with the economic problems of the transition period. . . . If we are not to lag behind actual practice, we must immediately proceed to tackle all these problems from the standpoint of the new situation. Otherwise it is impossible to overcome the bourgeois theories which are confusing the minds of our practical workers. Otherwise these theories, which possess the tenacity of prejudice, cannot be exterminated. It is only by combating the bourgeois prejudices in the field of theory that the position of Marxism-Leninism can be consolidated. Permit me to characterise at least a few of these bourgeois prejudices called theories, and to demonstrate their inadequacy in the light of certain cardinal problems of our reconstruction.

You know, of course, that the so-called theory of the "equilibrium" between the sectors of our national economy is still current among Communists . . .

It is not difficult to comprehend that this theory has nothing in common with Leninism. It is not difficult to comprehend that this theory objectively pursues the aim of defending the positions of individual peasant farming, of furnishing the kulak elements with a "new" theoretical weapon in their struggle against the collective farms. . . . And yet this theory is still current in our Press, and it cannot even be said that it is being seriously combated by our theoreticians, much less ruthlessly crushed. This inadequacy can only be explained by the backwardness of our theoretical thought.

And yet all that would have been necessary was to bring forth from the treasury of Marxism the theory of reproduction, to oppose this to the theory of equilibrium of the sectors—and not an atom of this theory would have been left. (*Leninism*, Vol. II, pp. 254-255.)

Why do our Marxist agrarian research workers not do this? Who benefits by the propagation of the ridiculous theory of "equilibrium" in our Press while the Marxist theory of reproduction is hidden under a bushel? (*Ibid.*, p. 256.)

We now come to a second prejudice of political economy, to a second theory of the bourgeois type. I refer to the theory of the "automatic development" of Socialist construction. This theory has nothing in common with Marxism; nevertheless it is being zealously propagated by our comrades in the Right camp . . .

Here we have another theory, the aim of which, objectively, is to furnish fresh weapons to the capitalist elements in the rural districts in their struggle against the collective farms. The anti-Marxist character of this theory is beyond all doubt. Is it not extremely strange that our theoreticians are not taking the trouble to extirpate this peculiar theory, which is causing so much confusion in the minds of our practical workers on the collective farms? (*Ibid.*, p. 257.)

Why, Stalin asks, have not the agricultural theorists gone into the "treasury" of Marxist theory and brought forth the "theory of reproduction"? The answer is, of course, that this theory was of no particular consequence until Stalin seized on it as a vehicle for his practical purposes and thus gave it significance.

The way in which the ability to "interpret" theory serves as an instrument of control stands out even more clearly when the technique is used to overcome opposition within the Party. In the passage quoted below Stalin uses a "shifting of classes," which he alone can perceive, as a means of discrediting the arguments of the opposition leaders.

What are our differences? What are they associated with? They are associated, first of all, with the shifting of classes that has been taking place of late in our country and in capitalist countries. Some comrades think that the differences in our Party are of a fortuitous nature. That is not true, comrades. That is absolutely not true. The differences within our Party have arisen on the basis of the shifting of classes, of the intensification of the class struggle, which has been taking place of late, and which is creating a turning-point in development. The principal error the Bukharin group commit is that they fail to see this shifting and this turning-point; they do not see them and neither do they want to see them. That, in fact, explains the failure to appreciate the new tasks of the Party and of the Comintern which is characteristic of the new opposition.

Have you observed, comrades, that in their speeches at the Plenum of the Central Committee and the Central Control Commission the leaders of the new opposition completely evaded the question of the shifting of classes in our country? They did not say a single word about the intensification of the class struggle and did not even remotely hint at the fact that our differences are associated precisely with this very intensification of the class struggle. They talked of everything, of philosophy and theory, but not a word did they say about the shifting of classes that determines the orientation and the practice of our Party at the present moment. How is this strange fact to be explained? Forgetfulness, perhaps? Of course not. Politicians cannot forget essentials. The explanation is that they neither see nor understand the new revolutionary processes going on both here, in our country, and in capitalist countries. The explanation is that they have overlooked the essential thing, they have overlooked the shifting of classes, which no politician has the right to overlook. That, in fact, explains the confusion and unpreparedness displayed by the new opposition in the face of the new tasks of our Party. (*Leninism*, Vol. II, p. 184.)

Why did not the members of the opposition speak of the shifting of classes, Stalin asks. The answer is, again, that not being psychic, they could have no way of knowing what Stalin would emphasize. Had they said something about a "shifting of classes" Stalin could just as easily have seized on any of a number of other points to treat as highly significant.

Since Marxist-Leninist theory is what the Dictator says it is, those who would engage in theoretical debate with him are trying to win a game the rules of which their opponent is free to make up as he goes along. Since he is invincible in the field of theory, the Dictator invariably moves the argument from the arena of practical policy to that of debate on the principles of Marxism-Leninism. To overcome all resistance he need only say that the theories to which the opposition adheres are non-Marxist in nature.

But when the Party assumed the offensive against the kulaks, and adopted emergency measures against them, the Bukharin-Rykov group threw off their mask and began to attack the Party policy openly. . . . In order to provide a theoretical backing for their case, they concocted the absurd "theory of the subsidence of the class struggle," maintaining, on the strength of this theory, that the class struggle would grow milder with every victory gained by Socialism against the capitalist elements. . . . In this way they tried to furbish up their threadbare bourgeois theory that the kulaks would peaceably grow into Socialism, and rode roughshod

over the well-known thesis of Leninism that the resistance of the class enemy would assume more acute
forms as the progress of Socialism cut the ground from
under his feet . . . (*History of the C.P.S.U.*, p. 293.)

All that Stalin does to discredit this argument is to depict
it as a "threadbare bourgeois theory." Since he has the power
to insist that his view shall prevail, the issue is settled. Note,
however, how clearly he perceives the technique used by the
opposition. "In order to provide a theoretical backing for
their case" they "concocted" a theory. The purpose of the op-
positionists came *first*, in other words, and the theory was
concocted or manufactured later to support and justify that
purpose. Bukharin and Rykov, taking a leaf out of Stalin's
book, dressed up their desire to pursue a more moderate
policy toward the "kulaks" in the robes of theory. Since
Stalin wields the power, however, it is his view that defines
orthodoxy.

It is said that Comrade Bukharin is the theoretician
of our Party. He is a theoretician, of course, and a
theoretician of no mean calibre. But, the fact is that
all is not well with his theorizing. That is evident if
only from the fact that he has piled up a whole heap
of errors on questions of Party policy, such as I have
just described. All these errors—errors with regard to
the Comintern; errors on questions of class struggle; of the intensification of the class struggle; questions of the peasantry, of N.E.P., of the new forms of
smychka—all these errors cannot be of a chance character. No, these errors are not of a chance character. These errors of Comrade Bukharin's arose out of
his false position, out of the gaps in his theories.
Comrade Bukharin is a theoretician, but he is not altogether a Marxian theoretician; he is a theoretician who
has much to learn in order to become a complete
Marxian theoretician. (*Leninism*, Vol. II, p. 221.)

Throughout the struggle the pretense is maintained that the argument revolves around points of "theory" rather than around the policies which the theory is being used to justify. In terming Bukharin's views "errors" Stalin is merely trying to give his own views the appearance of objective validity. The element of subjectivity is studiously ignored. Those who disagree with the Dictator are always objectively in error. When they are made to recant, they admit their "errors" and "mistakes," and apologize for the "incorrect" opinions which they have been guilty of holding. The fiction is maintained that there is a precise, definable body of Marxist-Leninist doctrine in existence. Since the Dictator is accepted as the interpreter of that body of doctrine, he is able to present all views differing from his own as deviations from Marxism-Leninism. Instead of it appearing that the Dictator arbitrarily condemns all who venture to disagree with him, it appears that he is merely making objective statements of fact when he holds certain views to be deviations from Marxism-Leninism.

The whole elaborate apparatus surrounding "deviation" exists to serve the same purpose, to veil the use of coercion and cause its application to appear less arbitrary than it actually is. Deviation from the Party line is treated as a great evil since it is a denial of Party discipline and Party unity.

It follows from this that the existence of fractions within the Party is directly inimical to unity and discipline. Obviously such fractions can only lead to the setting up of several centres of direction. The existence of several centres means a lack of one general controlling body; it means division of purpose, divided will; it means a weakening and an undermining of discipline, a weakening and an undermining of the dictatorship. (*Leninism*, Vol. I, p. 172.)

Party discipline is important because without it the Party could not have achieved its initial victories and could have no hope of achieving further victories in the future.

In fierce battle our Party forged the unity and solidarity of its ranks. And by unity and solidarity it achieved victory over the enemies of the working class. (Stalin, "On the Death of Lenin," reprinted in *The Essentials of Lenin*, Vol. I, p. 21.)

Certainly, almost everyone now realizes that the Bolsheviks could not have maintained themselves in power for two and a half months, let alone two and a half years, unless the strictest, truly iron discipline had prevailed in our Party . . . (*The Essentials of Lenin*, Vol. II, p. 573.)

This is what Party discipline should be like during the struggle for the establishment of the dictatorship of the proletariat.

Even more appropriate are the above-quoted words when we consider the conditions of affairs after the inauguration of the dictatorship. (*Leninism*, Vol. I, pp. 171-172.)

There are two kinds of deviation from this ideal Party discipline, the "Left" deviation and the Right or "opportunist" deviation. Both lead to the same evil results, but they approach them from opposite directions.

There cannot be the slightest doubt that the triumph of the Right deviation in our Party would release the forces of capitalism, would undermine the revolutionary position of the proletariat, and increase the chances of the restoration of capitalism in our country.

Where does the danger of the "Left" (Trotskyist) deviation in our Party lie? In the fact that it *overestimates* the strength of our enemies, the strength of capitalism. . . . There can be no doubt that the triumph of the "Left" deviation in the Party would result in the working class being sundered from its peasant base, and the vanguard of the working class from the more backward working-class masses, and consequently in the defeat of the proletariat and the improvement of the conditions for the restoration of capitalism.

We therefore see that both the dangers, the "Left" and the "Right," both the deviations from the Leninist line, the Right and the "Left," lead to the same results although from different directions. (Stalin, "The Right Danger in the C.P.S.U." reprinted in *Leninism*, Vol. II, pp. 145-146.)

Because both types of deviation lead to the same results, it does not, however, follow that they are indistinguishable.

It may be asked: If the "Left" deviation is in essence the same as the Right, opportunist, deviation, then where is the difference between them and where do you get the fight on two fronts? And indeed, if the victory of the Rights would mean increasing the chances of the restoration of capitalism, and if the victory of the "Lefts" would lead to exactly the same results, what is the difference between them and why is one called Right and the other "Left"? And if there is a difference, what does it consist in? Is it not true that both deviations spring from the same social root and that both are petty bourgeois deviations? . . .

The difference consists in the fact that their platforms are different, their demands are different, and their approach and methods are different. If, for instance, the Rights say, *"It is a mistake to build Dnieperstroy,"* while the "Lefts" on the contrary, say, *"What is the good of one Dnieperstroy? Give us a Dnieperstroy every year"* (laughter), it must be admitted that there is some difference between them. . . . If the Rights say, *"The difficulties have set in, is it not time to quit?"* while the "Lefts" on the contrary, say, *"What are difficulties to us: a fig for difficulties, let us dash ahead"* (laughter), it must be admitted that apparently there is some difference between them. (Stalin, *Leninism*, Vol. II, pp. 174-175.)

The nature of the Right and "Left" deviations is clear only in broadest outline since the Dictator gives the terms specific content as he goes along. A "Left" deviationist is any person who advocates a policy that in any way appears more extreme or more Marxist than the policy favored by the Dictator. A Right deviationist is any person who advocates a policy more moderate than that favored by the Dictator. These two types of deviation serve as the Scylla and Charybdis between which every Communist must make his way. To veer to one side or the other is to bring the movement to ruin. The only way to escape being a deviationist, and thus endangering the movement, is to be a perfect Marxist-Leninist, that is, to agree with the Dictator, the spokesman of Marxist-Leninist theory, at every point.

A certain embarrassment arises in connection with the "Left" deviation, however, that does not arise in connection with the Right. To be a Rightist is a "bad" thing in the Marxian universe and to be Left is "good." The Dictator is able, consequently, to deal with any persons he can present as Rightist merely by claiming that he is more Left or radical or revolutionary than they. But, by the same token, his own authority is weakened by those who present themselves as even further to the Left than he.

And so you get a picture of the specific platform and the specific methods of the "Lefts." And that explains why the "Lefts" sometimes succeed in winning over a part of the workers by their high-sounding "Left" phrases and by depicting themselves as the most determined opponents of the Rights . . . (Stalin, *Leninism*, Vol. II, p. 175.)

When it is widely accepted by the members of a society that to be Left is good, the advantage lies with the group that can present itself as the most Left of all groups. Since the Dictator, as the possessor of political power, cannot be as much of an extremist as those doctrinaires not confronted with the task of governing, he becomes vulnerable to their charges of being insufficiently Left. How is this natural movement to an ever-greater extremism to be halted? How is the revolution to be prevented from consuming its children? With splendid audacity Stalin states that it is *impossible* to be more Left than he, more Left than Leninism.

> But if the Trotskyist deviation is a "Left" deviation, does that not mean that the "Lefts" are more Left than the Leninists? No, it does not. Leninism is the most Left (without quotation marks) tendency in the world working class movement. (*Ibid.*, p. 175.)

In advancing this line of thought Stalin brings to their logical conclusion the ideas presented by Lenin in his pamphlet illuminatingly entitled *"Left Wing" Communism, An Infantile Disorder.* Not only does Stalin claim that his is the most Left movement in the world, he states that those who claim to be more Left than he are actually Rights in disguise.

> In our own Party we Leninists are the *only* Lefts (without quotation marks).... And in our Party we fight not only those whom we call open opportunist deviationists, but also those who want to be more "Left" than Marxism, more "Left" than Leninism, and conceal their right opportunist nature behind high-sounding Left phrases. Everybody understands that when people who had not rid themselves of Trotskyist tendencies are called "Left" it is meant ironically. Lenin referred to the "Left Communists" as Lefts, sometimes with, and sometimes without quotation marks. But everyone knows that Lenin referred to them as Lefts ironically and thereby emphasized that they were Left only in words, in appearance, but that in actual fact they represented petty-bourgeois Right tendencies. (*Ibid.*, pp. 175-76.)

> And we say that wherever there is a Right deviation there must be a "Left" deviation. The "Left" deviation is the shadow of the Right deviation. Lenin said . . . that the "Lefts" are Mensheviks turned inside-out.

That is absolutely true. The same thing can be said of the present day "Lefts." Those who incline toward Trotskyism are, in fact, Rights turned inside-out, they are Rights concealing themselves behind "Left" phrases. (*Ibid.*, p. 174.)

By making use of his position as supreme spokesman of Marxist theory, Stalin is enabled at one stroke to establish his monopoly of Leftism and to place the Left opposition on the only grounds where they can be attacked.

Not only is it bad to deviate from Marxism-Leninism in any way, i.e. to disagree with Stalin, but it is also bad to defend those who so deviate.

There are people in our Party who are prepared, in order to soothe their conscience, to subscribe to the fight against the Right danger, just in the same way as priests cry Halleluja! Halleluja! But they will not do a thing, not one practical thing, to fight the Right deviation as it should be fought, and overcome it. That sort of tendency we call a *conciliationist* tendency toward the Right, frankly opportunist, deviation. Obviously, the fight against conciliationism is an integral part of the general fight against the Right deviation and the Right danger. (*Leninism*, Vol. II, pp. 147-148.)

The point is that when war is declared on the Right deviation, the Right deviationists usually assume the colours of conciliators and place the Party in a difficult position. In order to forestall this manoeuvre of the Right deviationists we must insist on a determined fight against conciliationism. (*Ibid.*, p. 193.)

This doctrine of "conciliationism" is important only as another example of the way in which the Dictator is able to use his ability to manufacture "theory" to his own advantage. A "conciliationist" is anyone who refuses to join the fight against the danger that confronts the Party. The "danger" that Stalin wants to see fought is, of course, freedom to disagree with him. Nor can this submission to the will of the Dictator be merely of a general nature. There must be obedience at every point.

Hence, to belittle the Socialist ideology *in any way, to turn away from it in the slightest degree* means to strengthen bourgeois ideology. (*Essentials of Lenin*, Vol. I, p. 177.)

Whoever weakens ever so little the iron discipline of the party of the proletariat (especially during the time of its dictatorship) actually aids the bourgeoisie against the proletariat. (*Ibid.*, Vol. II, pp. 589-590.)

The conception of a loyal opposition is wholly foreign to this view. Within the Party there must be a "unity of wills." All Party members, that is, must submit to the single will of the Dictator.

The Party constitutes a unity of wills which is incompatible with any setting up of fractions and any division of power. (*Leninism*, Vol. I, p. 172.)

The possibility of agreement on ends and disagreement on means to those ends is ruled out. It is never admitted that the members of the opposition may be opposing Stalin's leadership precisely *because* they have the interests of the Party at heart.

Why? Because the struggle which the opposition is carrying on is essentially a struggle against the Party, a struggle against the regime of the proletarian dictatorship, with which certain non-proletarian sections cannot but be dissatisfied. The opposition reflects the dissatisfaction of the non-proletarian section of the population with the proletarian dictatorship and their pressure exerted upon it. (*Leninism*, Vol. II, p. 87.)

Those who disagree with the Dictator on any point are viewed as saboteurs of the Party and traitors to the class. They are assumed not to believe in the cause of the "proletariat" and to be actively trying to hinder it.

Can we carry on a successful struggle against our

class enemies without at the same time fighting deviations in our Party, and overcoming those deviations? No, it is impossible. It is impossible because we cannot develop a real struggle against our class foes while we have in our rear their reflection in the Party, while we leave in our rear people who do not believe in our cause and try in every way to hinder our progress. (*Leninism*, Vol. II, p. 391.)

Not only does Stalin call the members of the opposition enemies of the Party, he inflicts an even greater indignity on them. The same undermining attack that is used so effectively on enemies outside the Party is now turned on those persons inside the Party who balk at accepting Stalin's dictatorship.

It would be ridiculous to think that the resistance of these classes would not find some reflection in the ranks of our Party. And it actually did find reflection. The resistance of the disappearing classes is reflected by the various deviations from the line of Leninism which occur in the ranks of our Party. (*Ibid*., pp. 390-391.)

These petty-bourgeois groups crowd into the Party by one means or another, and bring with them a spirit of vacillation and opportunism, of disintegration and mistrust. They are mainly responsible for the creation of fractions within the Party, for the falling away of members, for disorganisation in our ranks, and for the endeavor to break up the Party from within. To do battle against imperialism with such "allies" as these is to lay oneself open to attack from two sides at once. (*Leninism*, Vol. I, p. 173.)

Stalin explains that the members of the opposition think as they do because they are the reflection within the Party of the class enemies of the proletariat. The advantage of attacking the members of the opposition in this fashion is that it allows Stalin to ignore or reject out of hand the problems and questions that they raise. By revealing the alleged "class origin" of their thinking he discredits what they say without ever having to consider it on its merits.

Not only are the opinions of the members of the opposition discredited by this tactic but those persons themselves, since they are asserted to be representative of the enemy, cease to be deserving of any concern. The ground is thus laid by the Dictator for the imposition of the ultimate sanction in his efforts to get "unity of will"—the creation of a "dangerous situation" for those who dare disagree with him.

Recently, Comrade Rykov was at the Party Conference in the Urals. He had, consequently, the most favorable occasion for correcting his mistakes, but what did we find? Instead of openly and resolutely breaking with his vacillations, he began there to twist and manoeuvre. Naturally, the Urals Conference was bound to give him a rebuff. Now compare Comrade Rykov's speech at the Urals Conference with his speech at the Sixteenth Congress. There is a wide gulf between them. There he twists and manoeuvres fighting the Conference. Here he tries openly and publicly to admit his mistakes, tries to break with the Right opposition, and promises to support the Party in the struggle against deviations. Whence comes such a change and how can it be explained? It is to be explained, apparently, by the dangerous situation which had been created in the Party for the former leaders of the Right opposition. It is not to be surprised at, therefore, that the Congress should form the definite opinion that, until you bring pressure to bear on these people, you will get nothing out of them. (Laughter and prolonged applause.) (*Leninism*, Vol. II, pp. 411-412.)

Or Comrade Tomsky, for example. He was lately in Tiflis, at the Transcaucasian Party Congress. Consequently he had a chance of atoning for his sins. And what happened? In his speech there he dealt with the

Soviet farms, the collective farms, co-operation, the cultural revolution and everything else of that kind, but did not say a word about the main thing, namely, his opportunist work in the Central Council of Trade Unions. And that is called fulfilling the pledges given to the Party! He wanted to outwit the Party, failing to understand that millions of eyes are watching every one of us and it is impossible to fool anyone in such conditions. Now compare his speech at Tiflis with his speech at this Congress, where he frankly and openly admitted his opportunist mistakes in the leadership of the C.C.T.U. There is a wide gulf between them. How is the difference to be explained? By the same dangerous situation which had grown up around the former leaders of the Right opposition. (*Leninism*, Vol. II, pp. 412-413.)

Lenin and Stalin, like the Gentlemen in Samuel Butler's Hudibras,

> . . . prove their doctrine orthodox
> By apostolic blows and knocks.

The effectiveness of the coercion is testified to by the absence of open opposition within the Party.

I said in my report that the Sixteenth Congress of the Party is one of the few Congresses in the history of our Party at which there is no opposition organized to any degree or capable of putting forward its own line of policy in opposition to the line of the Party. And that, as you see, is what proved to be the case. Not only has there been no organised opposition at our Congress, at the Sixteenth Party Congress, but there has not been even a small group, not even individual comrades, who thought fit to come out on the platform and say that the Party policy is wrong. It is clear that the line of policy of our Party is the only correct line, and its correctness turns out to be so obvious and indisputable that even the former leaders of the Right opposition thought it necessary unhesitatingly to emphasize in their speeches the correctness of the whole policy of the Party. (*Leninism*, Vol. II, pp. 405-406.)

At the Fifteenth Party Congress it was still necessary to prove that the Party line was right and to wage a struggle against certain anti-Leninist groups; and at the Sixteenth Party Congress the last adherents of these groups had to be despatched. At this Congress, however, there is nothing to prove and perhaps, no one to beat. Everyone now sees that the line of the Party has conquered. (Loud applause.) (*Socialism Victorious*, New York: International Publishers, 1935, pp. 61-62.)

Within the Soviet Union Marxist-Leninist theory serves two principal functions. It provides the series of doctrines by means of which the Dictator seeks to justify his rule and to bind the Russian people to himself and to his instrument, the Communist Party. Secondly, when extended to minor matters, it serves as a vehicle for countless day-to-day practical decisions that must be made. Each decision, no matter how trivial, is clothed in the garb of theory in an effort to impart to it the aura of sanctity that adheres to the basic Marxist propositions. Virtually everything that is done or left undone in the Soviet Union is justified in terms of "theory." Those activities presented as in accord with Marxist-Leninist theory are legitimate, while those not so presented are without justification and must be forbidden. The Dictator, as interpreter-creator of theory, is, consequently, in a position to exert enormous leverage on all aspects of society. He can control the foreign and domestic policies of the Soviet Union as well as determine the entire content of its culture, its literature, drama, music, philosophy, and science.

Anything is good Marxist-Leninist theory so long as the propagator can back up his position with power. This does not mean, however, that theory is unimportant or that it should not be studied. It is significant, though its significance is not that usually attributed to it. The intrinsic value of official theorizing is usually nil, but if that theorizing can be properly understood and interpreted, it is often extremely illuminating. The chapter that follows will seek to illustrate this in connection with the doctrine of "class consciousness."

Chapter VII

Class Consciousness: A Fiction and its Uses

COMMUNIST political thought assumes that each class possesses a will, a class will. In the following passages for example, the millions of persons in France and Great Britain who are thought to compose the bourgeoisie, are portrayed as following identical lines of reasoning and as arriving, without consultation, at identical conclusions.

In reality, the object of the struggle of the British and French bourgeoisie is to seize the German colonies and to ruin a competing nation which is distinguished for its more rapid economic development . . .

Neither of the two groups of belligerent countries lags behind the other in robbery, atrocities and the infinite brutalities of war; but in order to fool the proletariat and distract its attention from the only real war of liberation, namely, a civil war against the bourgeoisie both of "its own," and of "foreign" countries, in order to further this lofty aim, the bourgeoisie of each country is trying with the help of lying talk about patriotism to extol the significance of its "own" national war and to assert that it is not striving to vanquish the enemy for the sake of plunder and the seizure of territory, but for the sake of "liberating" all other peoples, except its own. (*Essentials of Lenin*, Vol. I, p. 620.)

This devious logic is pursued not by several million minds but by a single collective mind, or, what amounts to the same thing, a prototype class mind multiplied millions of times.

The very conception of a "dictatorship of the proletariat" is based on this class will assumption. Only if the proletariat, presumably composed of millions of persons, is believed to possess a single will can it be expected to "dictate." Like Marx and Engels, Lenin and Stalin frequently write as if great masses of individuals can act in unison on detailed and complex matters without having any need for organization or administrative agencies.

> But the organ of suppression is now the majority of the population, and not a minority, as was always the case under slavery, serfdom, and wage-slavery. And since the majority of the people *itself* suppresses its oppressors, a "special force" for suppression is *no longer necessary!* In this sense the state *begins to wither away.* Instead of the special institutions of a privileged minority (privileged officialdom, the command of the standing army), the majority itself can directly fulfill all these functions, and the more the functions of state power devolve upon the people generally the less need is there for the existence of this power. (*Essentials of Lenin*, Vol. II, p. 169.)

According to this class will strand of Communist thought the class requires no executive agency, no state, since it can itself perform all the tasks, however intricate and detailed, that must be performed. By virtue of the assumption that all members of the proletariat are animated in all particulars by a single class will, Lenin is able to maintain that complete self-government can exist. The proletariat "itself" is to assume the duties of governing and thus the dualism of rulers and ruled is to be overcome. Despite this Marxian assumption, the sovereign will by means of which the class is supposed to govern itself is nowhere to be found. It is no more than a fiction.

So long as the question remains primarily one of theory, as with Marx and Engels, the non-existence of the class will causes no inconvenience. When attempts are made to apply this theory to reality, however, the defect becomes important. Good or bad, democratic or tyrannical, a state mechanism of some kind is indispensable to a society of any size. The functions of organization and leadership must be provided for. Since the class will strand of Marxist thought makes no provision for these necessary functions, that basically unworkable theory must, when applied in practice, be supplemented by a theory which *will* provide for them. The vacuum created by the denial of the state and the non-existence of the class will must be filled. The theory of the Party, existing alongside the class will theory and in contradiction to it, meets that need. It is to the exploration of the theory of the Party, then, that this chapter will be devoted.

Most expositions of Marxist thought deal with the economic interpretation of history, the doctrine of classes, class warfare and so on, without ever touching on the Marxian treatment of the Communist Party. This oversight is understandable. Marx and Engels dealt so little with the Party that the significance of what they said when they did mention it has gone unnoticed. The following passage from Part II of the *Communist Manifesto* is little known but in terms of its implications for the future development of the Communist movement it is perhaps the most significant thing Marx and Engels ever wrote. In it the Communist Party is presented as the spokesman of the interests of the class, as the interpreter of the class will.

In what relation do the Communists stand to the proletarians as a whole?

The Communists do not form a separate party opposed to other working-class parties . . .

They have no interests separate and apart from those of the proletariat as a whole . . .

The Communists are distinguished from the other working class parties by this only: 1. In the national struggles of the proletarians of the different countries, they point out and bring to the front the common interests of the entire proletariat, independently of all nationality. 2. In the various stages of development which the struggle of the working classes against the bourgeoisie has to pass through, they always and everywhere represent the interests of the movement as a whole.

The Communists, therefore, are on the one hand practically the most advanced and resolute section of the working class parties of every country, that section which pushes forward all others; on the other hand, theoretically, they have over the great mass of the proletariat the advantage of clearly understanding the line of march, the conditions, and the ultimate general results of the proletarian movement. (*Communist Manifesto*, pp. 334-35.)

Though far from typical of the writings of Marx and Engels, this passage does nevertheless show that both strands of thought, the class will theory and the theory of the Party, are to be found there. The inconsistency of the two elements is less striking in their writings than in those of Lenin and Stalin only because they mention the Party far less frequently. Marx and Engels were never confronted with the organizational and administrative problems with which Lenin and Stalin have had to deal, so that they were never compelled to elaborate the theory of the Party. They were able, on the whole, to stay on the level of the class will in their propaganda and agitation without ever having to answer the embarrassing question of how the class will was to be known.

Two main claims are made for the Communists in the passage quoted above. First, they are said to represent "the common interests of the entire proletariat," to "always and everywhere represent the interests of the movement as a whole." Second, they are said to have over the great mass of the proletariat "the advantage of clearly understanding the line of march, the conditions, and the ultimate general results of the proletarian movement." These are the two component parts of the Marxian conception of "class consciousness"—

knowledge of the class will and understanding of history's laws.

The workings of "class consciousness" are never illustrated or explained by Marx and Engels because they cannot be illustrated or explained. Psychologically and physiologically speaking "class consciousness" is a fiction. There is no sixth sense represented by an awareness of class. There is no instinct revealing the mystical importance of "class." Wisdom, consequently, lies not in attempting to find some reality corresponding to this conception but in an effort to understand the role that the doctrine plays in the Marxist-Leninist scheme.

Class consciousness, as understood by Marx and Engels and Lenin and Stalin, is a fiction, but the importance of the idea is nevertheless great. It provides the justification for the Communist Party's assumption of the role of spokesman of the class will. Why should the Communist Party be accepted as speaking for the entire class? The Communist Party should be so accepted, comes the reply, because it is "class conscious," because, that is to say, the Communists always represent the interests of the class and because they know what History is going to do next. Class consciousness is the doctrine used to embody the class will in a concrete institution, the Communist Party. It is the doctrine that defines the Communist Party as the only organization capable of perceiving the "real interests" of the proletariat. It is the means by which the sovereignty of the class is denied in the very breath in which it is proclaimed.

And yet the movement was there, instinctive, spontaneous, irrepressible. Was not this just the situation in which a revolution had to succeed, led certainly by a minority, but this time not in the interests of the minority, but in the real interests of the majority? If, in all the longer revolutionary periods, it was so easy to win the great masses of the people by the merely plausible and delusive views of the minorities which are thrusting themselves forward, how could they be less susceptible to ideas which were the truest reflex of their economic position, which were nothing but the clear, comprehensible expression of their needs, of needs not yet understood by themselves, but only vaguely felt? . . . But here it was not a question of delusive views, but of giving effect to the very special interests of the great majority itself, interests, which at that time were certainly by no means clear to this great majority, but which must soon enough become clear in the course of giving practical effect to them, by their convincing obviousness. (Engels, Introduction to Marx's *Class Struggles in France*. London: Lawrence and Wishart, 1936, p. 16.)

Engels speaks here of a revolution led by a minority but in the interests of the majority. Who is to determine where the interests of this majority lie, however? Clearly not the majority itself, since it is explicitly stated that the majority is not clear as to where its interests lie. Engels speaks of "needs not yet understood by themselves, but only vaguely felt," and states that the interests of the majority "at that time were certainly by no means clear to the great majority." While the *majority* does not know where its interests lie, apparently a particularly qualified *minority* does know.

If the majority is not the best judge of where its interests lie, how can it ever be certain that the minority will really pursue those interests? The majority can have no certainty on this vital point other than the assurance of the minority itself. Twice in this passage Engels speaks of the ease with which minorities have in the past pursued their own interests while claiming to pursue those of the majority. What is to prevent this occurring in the case of the Communist revolution? Only the mystical doctrine of "class consciousness" stands in the way—a fiction invented and perpetuated by the minority to justify its role *vis-à-vis* the majority. Yet on the basis of this fiction the minority is apparently prepared to go ahead, trusting that the majority will soon recognize its interests "in the course of giving practical effect" to them. The minority is prepared to press forward and secure what it conceives to be the interests of the majority, *in spite of the majority*. The majority is to be "forced to be free."

These implications of the Marxian conception of the Party-class relationship were little developed by Marx and Engels. By Lenin and Stalin they have been so fully elaborated as to obliterate virtually all other elements in the Marxian system. No more than Marx or Engels do Lenin and Stalin try to demonstrate the existence of "class consciousness" or to explain its workings. In spite of the fact that the role attributed to the Party hinges on the validity of this conception, Lenin and Stalin prefer to assume rather than to demonstrate its existence.

The doctrine of class consciousness became of more than academic interest with Lenin's famous article *What is to be Done*, written in 1902. In that article Lenin advanced the thesis that there are two types of consciousness, "trade union consciousness" and the higher "Social-Democratic consciousness." The mass of workers could, he said, pass beyond the lower form only with the guidance of the Russian Social-Democratic Party, the Party to which Lenin and his followers belonged until the Bolshevik-Menshevik split.

> We said that *there could not yet be* Social-Democratic consciousness among the workers. This consciousness could only be brought to them from without. The history of all countries shows that the working class, exclusively by its own effort, is able to develop only trade union consciousness . . . (*Essentials of Lenin*, Vol. I, p. 170.)

According to this doctrine the Party is not merely representative of the class in the usual sense of that word, it is the "vanguard" of the class. It is more class conscious than the class itself.

> We are the Party of a class. . . . But it would be

Manilovism and "khvostism" to think that at any time under capitalism the entire class, or almost the entire class would be able to rise to the level of consciousness and activity of its vanguard, of its Social-Democratic guard and the whole of the masses which gravitate towards it, to forget the constant duty of the vanguard to *raise* ever wider strata to this most advanced level . . . (*Essentials of Lenin*, Vol. I, p. 299.)

The Party differs from other detachments of the working class primarily by the fact that it is not an ordinary detachment, but the *vanguard* detachment, a *class-conscious* detachment, a Marxist detachment of the working class armed with a knowledge of the life of society, of the laws of its development and of the laws of the class struggle, and for this reason able to lead the working class and to direct its struggle. (*History of the C.P.S.U.*, p. 46.)

Since it is on a higher level than the class as a whole, the Party is able to know the interests of the class better than the class itself can know them.

The immediate task that confronts the class-conscious vanguard of the international labour movement, i.e., the Communist Parties, groups, and trends, is to be able *to lead* the broad masses (now, for the most part, slumbering, apathetic, hidebound, inert and dormant) to their new position, or, rather, to be able to lead *not only* their own party, but also these masses, in their approach, their transition to the new position. (*Essentials of Lenin*, Vol. II, p. 627.)

It is the duty of the Party to lead the masses to their "new position." How is it determined that the masses have a "new position"? Certainly the "broad masses" did not decide this, since they are acknowledged to be "slumbering, apathetic, hidebound, inert, and dormant"—presumably in some old position. They have a "new position" only because the Party, in the wisdom of its class consciousness, has so decided. According to Lenin, the Party must arouse the masses from slumber, inform them that they have a new position, and lead them to it.

Since the Party possesses this characteristic of being "class conscious" it should not content itself with registering the desires of the masses but should convince the masses that it knows better than they where their interests lie.

> The Party is no true Party if it limits its activities to a mere registration of the sufferings and thoughts of the proletarian masses, if it is content to be dragged along in the wake of the "spontaneous movement" of the masses, if it cannot overcome the inertia and the political indifference of the masses, if it cannot rise superior to the transient interests of the proletariat, if it is incapable of inspiring the masses with a proletarian class consciousness. The Party should march at the head of the working class, it should see farther than the latter, it should lead the proletariat and not lag in the rear. (*Leninism*, Vol. I, p. 162.)
>
> For the whole task of the Communists is to be able to *convince* the backward elements . . . (*Essentials of Lenin*, Vol. II, p. 597.)
>
> You must not sink to the level of the masses, to the level of the backward strata of the class. That is incontestable. You must tell them the bitter truth. You must call their bourgeois-democratic and parliamentary prejudices—prejudices. (*Ibid.*, p. 600.)

The Communists are always termed the "advanced elements" while those who disagree with them are the "backward elements." In cases of disagreement there is no hint that what is involved is a difference of opinion on a debatable matter. It is assumed that there is error involved and that the error is on the part of those who disagree with the Communists. Members of the Party must tell the masses the "bitter truth," i.e. that they are wrong and the Communists are right. The idea is that the Communists possess the truth while their opponents possess only prejudices. It is taken for granted that the Party's policy is correct and that the only question is whether or not the class is sufficiently advanced to perceive this fact.

The Party's claim to perceive the class will or class interest amounts, in practice, to a claim to perceive the real will or real interests of each individual proletarian since the class will is assumed to be identical with every proletarian's real will. The basically anti-democratic nature of this entire doctrine is evident. By means of it, the decision as to where the interests of the members of society lie is taken from the persons involved and lodged with the Party. The many are able to follow their interests, their long-run interests, only by doing exactly as the leaders of the Party command. One of the central problems of democratic thought—How are the interests and desires of the governed to be communicated to the governors?—is defined out of existence. There ceases to be any need for machinery to make the interests of the ruled known to the rulers since it is assumed beforehand that the rulers always know better than the ruled where the interests of the latter lie. Thus, in good Jacobin fashion, Lenin can assume, regardless of all evidence to the contrary, that the Communist Party has the backing of the people.

It is clear that all power must pass to the Soviets. It should be equally indisputable for every Bolshevik that the revolutionary proletarian power (or the Bolshevik power—which is now one and the same thing) is assured of the ardent sympathy and unreserved support of all the toilers and exploited all over the world in general, in the warring countries in particular, and among the Russian peasantry especially. There is no point in dwelling on these all too well known and long demonstrated truths. (*Essentials of Lenin*, Vol. II, p. 133.)

Let the toilers, therefore, remain confident and resolute! Our Party, the party of the Soviet majority, stands solid and united in defence of its interests and, as heretofore, behind our Party stands the millions of the workers in the cities, the soldiers in the trenches and the peasants in the villages . . . (*Ibid.*, p. 244.)

When I heard that, I said to myself . . . let hundreds of extremely loud voices shout at us, "dictators," "violators," and similar epithets. We know that another voice is rising from the masses; these masses say to themselves; now we need not be afraid of the man with the gun, because he protects the toilers and will be ruthless in suppressing the rule of the exploiters. This is what the people have realised . . . (*Selected Works*, Vol. VII. p. 273.)

Not only is the Party defined as always knowing the interests of the governed, it is defined as always *pursuing* those interests. We have seen the way in which Marx and Engels refer to the Communists as having "no interests separate and apart from those of the proletariat as a whole," as pointing out and bringing to the front "the common interests of the entire proletariat." These statements about the Party and its relation to the class are unqualified. It is not said that the Party *strives* to live up to its ideals, that it strives to have no interests apart from the proletariat. Instead, it is stated that it *has* no interests apart from those of the proletariat. It is not said that the Communists *try* to represent the interests of the proletarian movement as a whole but that they "always and everywhere" *do* represent those interests.

The identification of the real and ideal indulged in by Marx and Engels did not stop with their treatment of "class," "class members" and so on, but extended to their treatment of the Party. The actual Communist Party is assumed by them to possess all the attributes of the ideally representative organization portrayed in their theory. Lenin and Stalin make precisely this same identification. They, too, assume that the actual Communist Party possesses all the virtues of the ideal Party of Marxist theory. They, too, fail to distinguish the real from the ideal and move freely back and forth from one to the other.

> We need a *Party* . . . systematically pursuing a correct, revolutionary Bolshevik policy. Have we such a party? We have. Is its policy correct? It is. (*Leninism*, Vol. II. p. 420.)

> Hence the need for the creation of a new party, a revolutionary fighting party, bold enough to lead the proletariat forward into the struggle for the seizure of power, experienced enough to find a solution for all the complications arising out of the revolutionary situation, and flexible enough to be able to steer the revolutionary barque safely through the shoals.

> Without such a party it is useless to dream of overthrowing imperialism and installing the dictatorship of the proletariat.

> This new party is the Party of Leninism. (*Ibid.*, Vol. I, p. 162.)

> But it can be taken as fully proved that the Communists are the most loyal and boldest champions of the labour movement all over the world, including America. (*Ibid.*, Vol. II, p. 66.)

> The Party is an inalienable portion of the working class. (*Ibid.*, Vol. I, p. 164.)

This identification of the actual Party with Marx's ideal Party is important inasmuch as the Party, once it has seized power and established its political monopoly, becomes, for all practical purposes, the state.

> The Party cadres constitute the commanding staff of the Party; and since our Party is in power, they also constitute the commanding staff of the leading organs of state. After a correct political line has been worked out and tested in practice, the Party cadres become the decisive force in the work of guiding the Party and the State. (Stalin, *From Socialism to Communism in the Soviet Union*, p. 43.)

The intimate and representative relationship which is presumed to exist between the Party and the class becomes the relationship which is presumed to exist between the state and society.

> By its character, its program and its tactic, our government is a proletarian, communist, workers' government. No amount of quibbling can obscure this fact.
> . . . Our government's program and its practical labours are proletarian and communist; and, so far as there is any meaning in words, our government is, therefore, proletarian and communist . . .
> . . . Our government, though proletarian by its program and its practical labours, is at the same time a workers' and peasants' government.
> How do you account for this?
> Because the fundamental interests of the bulk of the peasantry are identically the same as those of the proletariat.
> Because, consequently, the interests of the peasants find complete expression in the program of the proletariat, in the program of the Soviet State. (*Leninism*, Vol. I, p. 315.)
> . . . in the U.S.S.R. the Communist Party guides the Government in the interests of the proletariat. (*Ibid.*, Vol. II, p. 50.)

It is not stated that the government *tries*, to the best of its ability, to act in the interests of the peasantry and the proletariat. It is stated flatly that the government *does* so act. Just as the Party is defined as always acting in the interests of the proletariat, so, now, the state is defined as always acting in the interests of the peasants and proletarians. Just as the real Party was assumed to be the ideal Party of Marxist theory, so the actual government of the Soviet Union is presented as the ideal proletarian government of Marxist theory. The state is, in this manner, given *carte blanche*, since, by definition, it can never act other than in the interests of the governed. All of its acts are, ipso facto, legitimate exercises of power.

The Party is held to represent the class, according to this mode of thought, not because its members have been elected at the polls in competition with the members of other parties, but because of the assumed existence of a mystical bond joining Party and people. The Party would be held to represent the proletariat though no one cast a ballot. The mechanics of election are used in the Soviet Union not because the leaders of that country are devoted to democratic principles or because Marxist theory makes their use mandatory, but simply in order that no possible means of legitimizing the Party's rule be overlooked. Mechanical representation plays no important part in Marxist-Leninist thought and could be dispensed with entirely without difficulty.

As long as the Party leaders can see to it that both theories of representation, the mystical and the mechanical, yield the same results, both will be used. When they are unable to rig an election, however, it is to be expected that they will reject the theory of mechanical representation in favor of their primary doctrine which never fails to show that the Party has the support of the people. In order to find a situation in which such a conflict existed it is necessary to return to the period before the Party had solidified its control of the country and had developed its plebescitary techniques. The dissolution of the Constituent Assembly shortly after the Bolshevik seizure of power provides such an example.

The election to this Assembly, held before the October putsch, showed the Communist Party to be very distinctly a minority party. This was taken by Lenin as evidence, not that the Bolsheviks were mistaken in their belief that they represented the "will of the people," but as conclusive proof that the election did not really represent the sentiments of the voters. Thus he speaks of a "discrepancy between the composition of the Constituent Assembly and the real will of the people. . . ." (Lenin, "Theses on the Constituent Assembly,"

Essentials, Vol. II, p. 249.) In view of this conflict, the claims of the Bolsheviks must have precedence over the merely "formal rights" of the Constituent Assembly.

The result of all the above-mentioned circumstances taken in conjunction is that the Constituent Assembly, summoned on the basis of party lists compiled before the proletarian-peasant revolution, and under the rule of the bourgeoisie, must inevitably clash with the will and interests of the toiling and exploited classes which on October 25 began the Socialist revolution against the bourgeoisie. Naturally, the interests of this revolution stand higher than the formal rights of the Constituent Assembly . . . (*Essentials of Lenin*, Vol. II, p. 249.)

The "crisis" could be painlessly resolved, said Lenin. only if the Assembly would capitulate and accept Bolshevik dictation.

The only chance of securing a painless solution of the crisis which has arisen owing to the divergence between the elections to the Constituent Assembly, on the one hand, and the will of the people and the interests of the toiling and exploited classes, on the other, is for . . . the Constituent Assembly to accept the law of the Central Executive Committee on these new elections, for the Constituent Assembly to proclaim that it unreservedly recognizes the Soviet power . . . (*Ibid.*, p. 250.)

Unless these conditions are observed, the crisis in connection with the Constituent Assembly can be settled only in a revolutionary way, by the Soviet power adopting the most energetic, rapid, firm and determined revolutionary measures against the Cadet-Kaledin counter-revolution no matter under what slogans and institutions (even membership of the Constituent Assembly) this counter-revolution may screen itself. Any attempt to tie the hands of the Soviet power in this struggle would be tantamount to aiding and abetting counter-revolution. (*Ibid.*)

When the Assembly did not capitulate, the Bolsheviks and Left-Socialist-Revolutionaries withdrew from it, maintaining that it was now they who "patently" enjoyed "the confidence of the workers and the majority of the peasants." (*Essentials of Lenin*, Vol. II, p. 268.)

> To relinquish the sovereign power of the Soviets, to relinquish the Soviet republic won by the people, for the sake of bourgeois parliamentarism and a Constituent Assembly, would now be a retrograde step and involve the complete collapse of the October workers' and peasants' revolution. (*Ibid.*, Vol. II, p. 268.)

"Accordingly," Lenin said, "the Central Executive Committee resolves: the Constituent Assembly is hereby dissolved." (*Ibid.*, p. 268.)

Faced with a contradiction between the evidence of the election and the Marxist dogma that the Communist Party always and everywhere is the true representative of the toiling masses, Lenin did not hesitate to reject the evidence in favor of the dogma.

This doctrine of mystical or "virtual" representation* can, of course, justify the rule of a single man, a *Führer* or a *Vozhd*, as easily as that of a group of men. The Party is presented as the mystical representative of the class and the leader as the mystical representative of the Party. Thus it fol-

---

*Virtual representation is that in which there is a communion of interests, and a sympathy in feelings and desires, between those people who act in the name of any description of people, and the people in whose name they act, though the trustees are not actually chosen by them. This is virtual representation. Such a representation I think to be, in many cases, even better than the actual. It possesses most of its advantages and is free from many of its inconveniences; it corrects the irregularities in the literal representation, when the shifting current of human affairs, or the acting of public interest in different ways, carry it obliquely from its first line of direction. The people may err in their choice; but common interest and common sentiment are rarely mistaken. (Edmund Burke, *Works*, London: Henry G. Bohn, 1855, Vol. III, pp. 334-335.)

lows that the will of a single individual, a dictator, may fulfill the will of a class.

The question has become one of really enormous significance: First, the question of principle, *viz.*, is the appointment of individual persons, dictators with unlimited powers, in general compatible with the fundamental principles of Soviet government? . . .

The irrefutable experience of history has shown that in the history of revolutionary movements the dictatorship of individual persons was very often the vehicle, the channel of the dictatorship of the revolutionary classes. . . . Hence, there is absolutely no contradiction in principle between Soviet (*i.e.*, socialist) democracy and the exercise of dictatorial powers by individual persons. (Lenin, *Selected Works*, Vol. VII, pp. 341-342.)

Since the doctrine of class consciousness gives the Communist Party a role of extreme importance it is understandable that Lenin and Stalin should combat any doctrine seeking to replace it. They cannot, for example, tolerate a doctrine proclaiming the importance of the free development of the labor movement.

There is a lot of talk about spontaneity, but the *spontaneous* development of the labour movement leads to its becoming subordinated to the bourgeois ideology . . . for the spontaneous labour movement is pure and simple trade unionism . . . and trade unionism means the ideological enslavement of the workers to the bourgeoisie. Hence, our task, the task of Social Democracy, is to *combat spontaneity,* to *divert* the labour movement from its spontaneous, trade unionist striving to go under the wing of the bourgeoisie, and to bring it under the wing of revolutionary Social-Democracy. (*Essentials of Lenin*, Vol. I, p. 177.)

Without the leadership of the Social-Democratic Party the labor movement can only result in the ideological enslavement of the workers to the bourgeoisie. The labor movement must, therefore, be saved from itself. It must be diverted from its normal course of development and be brought under the direction of the Bolsheviks.

The theory that we must bow our heads before the spontaneity of the working-class movement is the theory of those who are decisively opposed to an attempt to give the spontaneous movement a deliberate and purposive character; it is the theory of those who do not want our Party to march in front of the working class, stimulating the masses till they reach the level of conscious action, leading the movement. It is the theory of those who consider that the thinking elements should let the movement go its own way, that the Party should listen for the voice of the spontaneous movement and be content to trot along in the rear . . . (*Leninism*, Vol. I, p. 96.)

The theory of spontaneity is the theory of opportunism; the theory that we must bow before the spontaneity of the working-class movement; the theory which in practice amounts to a denial that the vanguard of the working class, the Party of the working class, can act as leader for the class as a whole. (*Ibid.*, p. 95.)

The "theory of spontaneity" is an object of attack because it represents a denial of Lenin's doctrine of class consciousness, because it denies to the Party the leading role that Lenin and Stalin wish it to have.

This chapter has sought to show the way in which the revolutionary aspect of Marxist political thought is destroyed when it is accepted, first, that the Communist Party should direct the proletariat and, second, that the proletariat has seized power in the Soviet Union and is now the ruling rather than the ruled class. When these doctrines are joined, Marxist theory is automatically converted from a doctrine advocating *resistance* to the powers that be into a doctrine preaching unconditional obedience and *submission* to the powers that be. In lands where the proletariat has not yet seized power, revolution continues to be taught. In those lands, however, where the "dictatorship of the proletariat" is assumed to exist, it is not revolution but unqualified submission that is taught.

CHAPTER VIII

The "Dictatorship of the Proletariat"

LENIN and Stalin have agreed that the "dictatorship of the proletariat" is the "tap root" of the revolution, the "fundamental question" of Leninism. (*Leninism*, Vol. I, p. 15.) This conception, however, implies the existence of a psychological impossibility, a class will. The dictatorship that exists cannot be that of a "class," it cannot be that of the proletariat. Whose, then, is it?

The answer is made evident by the preceding chapter. The political significance of the Marxian scheme is completely altered when the implications of Marx's theory of the Party are examined. A system of thought which appears to provide for absolute democracy and the unqualified sovereignty of the class is seen, instead, to provide for the unqualified subordination of the class to the Communist Party. By the simple expedient of embodying the fictitious class will in the institution of the Party, a super-democratic theory is converted into an instrument for tyranny. This chapter will examine a number of the techniques by means of which the Party achieves in practice the dictatorship provided for by theory. First, then, what is the relation of the Communist Party to the government?

Question II: *Is it correct to say that the Communist Party controls the Russian government?*

Reply: It all depends upon what is meant by control. In capitalist countries they have a rather curious conception of control. I know that a number of capitalist Governments are controlled by big banks, notwithstanding the existence of "democratic" parliaments. The parliaments assert that they alone control the

Governments. As a matter of fact, the composition of the Governments is predetermined, and their actions are controlled by great financial consortiums. . . . If such control is meant, then I must declare that control of the Government by money-bags is inconceivable and absolutely excluded in the U.S.S.R., if only for the reason that the banks have been nationalized long ago and the money-bags have been ousted. Perhaps the delegation did not mean control, but the guidance exercised by the Party in relation to the Government. If that is what the delegation meant by its question then my reply is: Yes, our Party does guide the Government. (Stalin, "Interview with the First American Labour Delegation in Russia," in *Leninism*, Vol. II, p. 48.)

In what is the guidance of the Government by the workers' Party in the U.S.S.R., by the Communist Party of the U.S.S.R., expressed . . . ?*

First of all it is expressed in that the Communist Party strives, through the Soviets and their Congresses, to secure the election to the principal posts in the Government of its own candidates, its best workers, who are loyal to the cause of the proletariat and prepared truly and faithfully to serve the proletariat. This it succeeds in doing in the overwhelming majority of cases because the workers and peasants have confidence in the Party. It is not an accident that the chiefs of the Government departments in this country are Communists and that these chiefs enjoy enormous respect and authority.

Secondly, the Party supervises the work of the administration, the work of the organs of power; it recti-

---

*By joining "workers' Party" and "Communist Party" with a comma and thus identifying them, Stalin begs the question as to whether or not the Communist Party *is* a workers party. The use of this question-begging technique is standard procedure with Lenin and Stalin. To avoid repetition, all further examples of it will be passed over without comment.

fies their errors and defects, which are unavoidable, it helps them to carry out the decisions of the Government and strives to secure for them the support of the masses. It should be added that not a single important decision is taken by them without the direction of the Party.

Thirdly, when the plan of work is being drawn up by the various Government organs, in industry or agriculture, in trade or in cultural work, the Party gives general leading instructions defining the character and direction of the work of these organs in the course of carrying out these plans. (*Ibid.*, p. 49.)

First, the Party succeeds in getting its candidates elected to the principal posts in the government. Secondly, it supervises the work of all governmental departments. The significance of this latter fact is made clear when it is stated, thirdly, that this covers work done "in industry or agriculture, in trade or in cultural work,"—in short, virtually all fields of activity that men normally engage in.

Nor is it only the departments of the government that the Party "guides." It controls the Komsomol, the Young Communist League also.

The Union of Young Communists is not, formally speaking, a section of the Party organisation. Nevertheless, it is a communist organisation. This means that the Union of Young Communists, without being in the formal sense a Party organisation of the workers and peasants, has to carry on its activities under the leadership of the Party. . . . Young Communists must always bear in mind that the most important part of the work of the Union of Young Communists is to ensure that the Party shall keep the lead. Young Communists must never forget that in default of such leadership, the Union of Young Communists will not be able to fulfill its fundamental task, that of educating the young workers and the young peasants in the spirit of the dictatorship of the proletariat and of communism. (*Leninism*, Vol. I, p. 345.)

Take the Komsomol (Young Communist League), which combines nearly two million young workers and peasants. Is it an accident that the overwhelming majority of the elected leading elements in the Young Communist League are Communists? I think that it cannot be said to be an accident. Thus you have another test of the strength and authority of the Communist Party. (*Ibid.*, Vol. II, p. 53.)

The Party guides the trade unions, the soviets, the cooperative societies, in the same fashion.

One of the Delegates: On the same principles the Party guides the trade unions?

Stalin: In the main, yes. Formally, the Party cannot give instructions to the trade unions, but the Party gives instructions to the Communists who work in the trade unions. It is known that in the trade unions there are Communist fractions as there are also in the Soviets, co-operative societies, etc. It is the duty of these Communist fractions to secure by argument the adoption of decisions in the trade unions, in the Soviets, co-operative societies, etc., which correspond to the Party's instructions. This they are able to achieve in the overwhelming majority of cases because the Party exercises enormous influence among the masses and enjoys their great confidence. (*Ibid.*, p. 50.)

The picture that emerges is unmistakably that of control by the Party of all organizations of any consequence in the Soviet Union. The Party represents, as the 1936 Constitution puts it, "the directing kernel of all organizations of toilers, both public and state." (Article 126.) That this control is not "formal" does not make it any the less effective.

But this does not mean that the non-Party organisations should be formally subject to the Party. All that is requisite is that the Party members who belong to

these organisations should use their influence and all
their arts of persuasion to bring these non-Party organisations into the closest proximity to the Party, and to
lead them to place themselves of their own free will
under the political guidance of the Party. (*Leninism*,
Vol. I, pp. 168-169.)

Achievement of this control of lesser associations is a fixed
policy, as is made evident by a provision of the Rules of the
Communist Party of the Soviet Union adopted at the 17th
Party Congress.

At all congresses, conferences and elective organs of
non-Party, Soviet, trade-union, co-operative and other
mass organisations in which there are not less than
three Party members, Party groups are organized
whose task it is to consolidate the influence of the
Party in every respect and to carry out its policy in the
non-Party environment, to strengthen the iron Party
and Soviet discipline, to struggle against bureaucracy
and to supervise the fulfilment of party and Soviet
directives. (*Socialism Victorious*, p. 708.)

Lenin and Stalin have, of course, provided a theoretical
justification for the Party's control of all lesser associations.

Its function [the Party's] is to *unify* the work of all
the mass organisations of the proletariat, without exception, and to *guide* their activities toward a single
end, that of the liberation of the proletariat. Unifica-
tion and guidance are absolutely essential. There must
be unity in the proletarian struggle; the proletarian
masses must be guided in their fight for power and
for the upbuilding of socialism; and only the proletarian vanguard, only the Party of the proletariat, is
competent to unify and guide the work of the mass
organisations of the proletariat. Nothing but the Party
of the proletariat, nothing but the Communist Party,
is able to act as universal leader in the system of the

dictatorship of the proletariat. (*Leninism*, Vol. I, p. 31.)

The proletariat is assumed to be engaged in a struggle the severity of which makes it necessary that there be unified leadership of all mass organizations of the class. This unifying and directing function is naturally given to the Party.

> But how can unity of command be achieved in the presence of such a diversity of organisations? How are we to guarantee that their multiplicity will not lead to confusion and disagreement in the guidance of the struggle? Some may contend that these organisations function only within a special sphere of activity, and that therefore they cannot hinder one another. Maybe so. But they must all direct their activities towards the same goal, for each of them serves the same class, the proletariat. It may well be asked, who decides upon the direction, the general direction all these organisations shall take? Where is the central unit of organisation which, because of its past experience, is not only capable of determining the line of activity these manifold organisations should take, but likewise wields sufficient authority to induce these organisations to keep within the prescribed lines in order to achieve unity of command and to avoid any possibility of confusion?
>
> This central unit of organisation is the Party. (*Leninism*, Vol. I, p. 168.)

There can be unity of purpose, Stalin assumes, only when there is a *total* absence of disagreement among the various organizations. The creation of this unanimity requires the imposition of a single will upon all other wills. "Where is the central unit of organisation which . . . wields sufficient authority to induce these organisations to keep within prescribed lines. . . . This central unit of organisation is the Party."

The advantages that accrue to the Party as a result of this

control of lesser associations are obvious. One of the greatest of these is suggested by a passage from Stalin's "Problems of Leninism."

What are these "belts" or "levers" in the system of the dictatorship of the proletariat? What is the "guiding force"? Why are they needed?

The levers and the belts are the mass organisations of the proletariat, without whose aid the dictatorship cannot be realised in practice.

* * *

The proletariat needs these belts, these levers, and this guiding force, because without them it would, in its struggle for victory, be like a weaponless army in the face of organised and armed capital. It needs these organisations, because without them it would inevitably be defeated in the fight for the overthrow of the bourgeoisie, for the consolidation of its own power, for the upbuilding of socialism. The systematic help of these organisations and of the guiding force of the workers' vanguard is indispensable, because otherwise the dictatorship of the proletariat could not be durable or steadfast. (*Leninism*, Vol. I, p. 29.)

When he states that without these belts and levers a durable and firm dictatorship would be impossible, Stalin speaks the truth. These various mass organizations are "levers" indeed. The description is an apt one. They are not, however, as Stalin suggests, the means by which the proletariat effects its dictatorship over society but, rather, the means used by the Party to move the bulk of the population. They serve, to use Stalin's term, as "links" between the Party on the one hand and the mass of individuals on the other.

To sum up: the *trade unions*, as mass organisations of the proletariat, linking the Party with the working class as a whole, especially in the industrial field; the *soviets*, as mass organisations of all who labour, linking the Party with these latter, especially in the political field; the *cooperatives* as mass organisations, chiefly of the peasants, linking the party with the peasant masses, especially in the economic field and as concerns peasant participation in the work of socialist construction; the *League of Youth*, as a mass organisation of the young workers and peasants, whose function it is to help the proletarian vanguard in the socialist education of the rising generation and in the formation of young reserves; finally, the *Party,* as the essential guiding force within the system of the dictatorship of the proletariat, and called upon to lead all the before-mentioned mass organisations ... (*Ibid.*, pp. 31-32.)

Lesser associations within a society are commonly regarded as barriers to state tyranny since they have, in time past, served as nuclei around which men interested in resisting the state could be gathered. In the Soviet Union, however, the various lesser associations are not barriers to state tyranny, but are means to it. Instead of prohibiting associations because they might become centers of resistance to Party demands, Party leaders permit them to exist but make certain that they are controlled.

The opportunists' theory of "independence" and of "neutrality" in respect of the non-Party organisations ... is, in the light of all these considerations, seen to be quite incompatible with the theory and practice of Leninism. (*Leninism*, Vol. I, p. 169.)

Instead of serving to limit to the authority of the state, all organizations in the Soviet Union are arms of the state. By controlling all legal associations the Party, at one stroke, denies to an opposition all possibility of organizing legally and, at the same time, takes into its own possession a potent means for exerting leverage on society. Instead of trying to eradicate the tendency of men to form groups, the Party makes use of it, acting on the principle that the best way to control men's thoughts and actions is to control the groups into which they gather.

The armed forces, always a potential source of opposition in a dictatorship, are controlled in the same fashion.

> The Red Army was victorious because its leading core, both at the front and in the rear, was the Bolshevik Party . . . (*History of the C.P.S.U.*, p. 245.)

The evils of a failure to maintain a strong "leading core" in the armed services are quite apparent to Stalin.

> Two circumstances facilitated the outbreak of the Kronstadt mutiny: the deterioration in the composition of the ships' crews, and the weakness of the Bolshevik organisation in Kronstadt. (*Ibid.*, p. 250.)

In all these groups the Party maintains its control by a judicious mixture of persuasion and coercion.

> In such circumstances, leadership means: ability to convince the masses that the Party policy is right; ability to issue and to act upon slogans that will bring the masses nearer to the Party standpoint, and will make it easier for them (as the outcome of their own experience) to realise the soundness of the Party policy; ability to raise the masses to the Party level, and thus to ensure their cooperation at the decisive hour. (*Leninism*, Vol. I, p. 45.)

> What do "consolidate" and "enlarge" signify in relation to the dictatorship of the proletariat? They mean that the proletarian masses must be imbued with the spirit of discipline and organisation; that the proletarian masses must be inoculated against the harmful influences of the petty-bourgeoisie, must be prevented from acquiring petty-bourgeois habits and customs . . . (*Leninism*, Vol. I, p. 170.)

The more thoroughly the masses are indoctrinated, the more thoroughly they are "inoculated" against ideas which the Party leaders believe to be harmful, the smaller is the amount of coercion that must be applied. Lenin and Stalin understood the effectiveness of propaganda, but they understood, further, that by itself it is seldom completely effective. What then is to be done with those who will not be persuaded?

What is to be done if the minority refuses to submit to the will of the majority? (*Ibid.*, p. 45.)

What is to be done with those who, after exposure to the full pressure of propaganda, continue to be opposed to the aims of the Party's leaders? This is the way the question must be re-stated, since the leaders of the Party always present their demands as either the demands of the majority or as the demands of every member of the class.

When the Party enjoys the confidence of the majority, may it and must it force the minority to comply? Yes, it may and it must. The fundamental way in which the Party acts upon the masses is by persuasion; it is by *persuading* the majority that the leadership is safeguarded. This however does not exclude compulsion. On the contrary, it presupposes the use of compulsion when compulsion is supported by the confidence of the majority of the working class ... (*Ibid.*, pp. 45-46.)

'We have applied force rightly and successfully in those cases in which we have paved the way for it by persuasion.' (Lenin)

This is perfectly correct for on no other supposition is leadership possible. (*Ibid.*, pp. 46-47.)

In spite of the unmistakable evidences of rigid Party dictatorship, Stalin, as Lenin before him, continues to speak of the Soviet Union as the "land where the dictatorship of the proletariat is in force . . ." (*Leninism*, Vol. I, p. 33.) By what techniques does he attempt to present the dictatorship of the Communist Party as the dictatorship of the proletariat? First of all, he denies that the "guidance" which the Party exercises amounts to dictatorship. He adduces, in fact, quite the contrary conclusion:

Take first of all the trade unions, which combine nearly ten million proletarians. Let us examine the composition of the leading organs of these trade unions. Is it an accident that Communists are at the head of these organs? Of course not. It would be absurd to think that the workers in the U.S.S.R. are indifferent to the composition of the leading organs of their trade unions.

The workers in the U.S.S.R. grew up and received their training in the storms of three revolutions. They learned, as no other workers learned, to try their leaders and expel them if they do not satisfy the interests of the proletariat. . . . And if these workers express their complete confidence in the Communists, elect them to responsible posts in the trade unions, it is direct evidence that the strength and stability of the Communist Party among the workers in the U.S.S.R. is enormous. This is one test of the undoubted sympathy of the broad masses of the workers for the Communist Party. (*Leninism*, Vol. II, pp. 52-53.)

Now examine the composition of the leading organs of our Soviets both in the centre and locally. Is it an accident that the overwhelming majority of the elected leading elements are Communists? Clearly, it is not an accident. Does not this fact prove that the Communist Party enjoys the confidence of millions of the masses of the peasantry? I think it does. This is another test of the strength and stability of the Communist Party. (*Ibid.*, p. 53.)

Acceptance of Party leadership by these organizations is regarded as indicating not that the Party dictatorship is effective, but rather that the peasants and proletarians have enormous faith and confidence in the Party.

In much the same way, the Party's monopoly of political activity is justified.

The position of our Party as the only legal Party in the country (the monopoly of the Communist Party) is not something artificial and deliberately invented. Such a position cannot be created artificially by administrative machinations, etc. The monopoly of our Party grew out of life, it developed historically as a result of the fact that the Socialist-Revolutionary Party and the Menshevik Party became absolutely bankrupt and departed from the stage of our social life. (*Ibid.*, p. 58.)

With great boldness and historical inaccuracy, Stalin suggests that the Socialist-Revolutionary and Menshevik parties "departed from the stage" of their own accord, unassisted by the Bolsheviks. The Communist Party's monopoly of legality is treated as a wholly natural development instead of as evidence of the effectiveness of the way in which it warred against all other parties in accord with Lenin's fixed ideas on this subject.

"The unity of the proletariat in the epoch of social revolution," Lenin says, "can be achieved only by the extreme revolutionary party of Marxism and only by a relentless struggle against all other parties." (Quoted by Stalin in *History of the C.P.S.U.*, p. 359.)

Marxist theory holds that there is to come to pass a dictatorship of a "class" called the proletariat. The Party is secure in its position only so long as it can pass off its dictatorship as the dictatorship of that class. It is secure only so long as it succeeds in having itself regarded as the mindless, selfless, instrument of the class. If the dictatorship that exists were to be seen as merely the dictatorship of the Party, that dictatorship would lose the sanction that Marxist theory gives it. For quite obvious reasons, then, Lenin and Stalin must insist that the dictatorship of the Party is the prophesied dictatorship of the class. They must insist on the identification of that which exists with that which was prophesied and must crush any attempt to distinguish the two.

> The mere presentation of the question—dictatorship of the Party *or* dictatorship of the class, dictatorship (Party) of the leaders, *or* dictatorship (Party) of the masses?—testifies to the most incredible and hopeless confusion of mind. These people are straining to *invent* something quite out of the ordinary, and, in their effort to be clever, make themselves ridiculous. (*Essentials of Leninism*, Vol. II, p. 587.)

Lenin seeks to laugh the matter out of court but the vehemence of his reaction suggests that he fully appreciates the explosive nature of the issue raised.

> To go so far in this connection as to contrast, in general, dictatorship of the masses to dictatorship of the leaders is ridiculously absurd and stupid. (*Ibid.*, p. 588.)

The dictatorship of the Party and the dictatorship of the class must not be *contrasted* lest the former appear as something other than the latter and be resisted in the name of the latter.

The "dictatorship of the proletariat" has been shown, in this chapter, to be nothing more than the dictatorship of the Communist Party. Since the Party has always been under the rule of a single man, first Lenin and now Stalin, the dictatorship of the class amounts in practice to the dictatorship of a single man. Instead of acknowledging this fairly obvious fact, however, Lenin and Stalin have sought to maintain the fiction that the "proletariat" rules in the Soviet Union, that the real is the achievement of the ideal. Since Lenin and Stalin have insisted that Communist practice is, in every respect, one with Marxist-Leninist theory, the distinction between theory and practice that has been made in this chapter may prove illuminating if applied to questions other than that of the dictatorship.

CHAPTER IX

Real and Ideal: I

THIS chapter and the one that follows will attempt to show
1) that Lenin and Stalin have made a systematic effort to
identify those things which exist with those things which,
according to Marxist and Marxist-Leninist theory, should exist, and 2) that attempts to effect this identification have
involved them in a wholesale falsification of reality. The
present chapter will illustrate these points in connection with
the Communist treatment of the October Revolution and the
ambiguity that, in practice, surrounds the Communist use of
such terms as bourgeois, proletarian, and kulak.

The two revolutions of 1917 were events of tremendous
importance to the Communist movement. The first of these,
the February revolution, represents, in the Leninist view, the
overthrow of feudal society by the bourgeoisie.

> The state power in Russia has passed into the hands
> of a new *class*, namely, the bourgeoisie and landlords
> who had become bourgeois. *To that extent* the bour-
> geois-democratic revolution in Russia has been com-
> pleted. (*Essentials of Lenin*, Vol. II, p. 25.)

The second of the two revolutions, the October Revolution,
is supposed to represent the overthrow of this bourgeoisie by
the proletariat—the "proletarian revolution" foretold by
Marx. It is presented as the epoch-making conflict between
two mighty "classes," the proletariat and the bourgeoisie.

> Having completed the bourgeois-democratic revolu-
> tion in conjunction with the peasantry in general, the
> Russian proletariat passed on definitely to the Social-
> ist revolution . . . (*Ibid.*, p. 417.)

It is well known that, thanks to Lenin and his Party,
the idea of the hegemony of the proletariat was skill-

fully applied in Russia. This, in passing, explains the fact that the revolution in Russia brought the proletariat to power. In previous revolutions it usually happened that the workers did all the fighting at the barricades, shed their blood, and overthrew the old order, but power passed into the hands of the bourgeoisie, which later oppressed and exploited the workers. This was the case in England and in France. That was the case in Germany. In Russia, however, things took a different turn. (*Leninism*, Vol. II, pp. 45-46.)

Everything is supposed to have occurred exactly as was foretold.

Things have turned out just as we said they would. The course taken by the revolution has confirmed the correctness of our reasoning. (*Essentials of Leninism*, Vol. II, p. 414.)

Practice realizes theory. The reality is the achievement of the ideal.

What, then, is the second peculiarity of the October revolution?

It is that the October revolution is a model of the practical application of Lenin's theory of the proletarian revolution. (*Leninism*, Vol. I, p. 191.)

This identification of the actual revolution with the ideal proletarian revolution of Marxist theory was made possible only by Lenin's careful preparation. Before the revolution occurred Lenin had already (1) substituted his theory of revolution for Marx's and had, (2) advanced the idea that war accelerated the development of capitalism.

It was a fundamental tenet of Marx's theory of revolution that proletarian revolutions would occur first in the most industrialized countries. There the proletariat would be strong and capitalism weak. Lenin was a Russian as well as a Marxist, however, and he wanted to see a revolution take place in his industrially backward native land. Since a revolution in a non-industrialized country was directly contrary to Marx's theory, Lenin had either to modify Marx's theory in a thoroughgoing fashion or cease being a Marxist. The result was the development of his theory of imperialism.

(1) "Capitalism has become a world-wide system of colonial oppression and financial strangulation of most of the globe by a handful of 'advanced' countries." (Lenin)

(2) "Three world powers, the United States of America, Great Britain, and Japan, armed to the teeth, divide the 'spoils' and drag the world into the wars which their squabbles over the booty entail." (Lenin)

(3) The contradictions developing within the world-wide system of financial oppression, and the impossibility of avoiding a clash of arms, render international imperialism more vulnerable to the onslaught of the revolution and more liable to being broken up in certain lands.

(4) Such a break-up of the imperialist front is more likely to take place in countries where imperialism is less strongly entrenched, less stabilised, and where, consequently, the revolution can develop more easily.

(5) In view of all this, the victory of socialism in one country alone is possible and probable, *even though that country is in a backward state of development* in regard to capitalism, and even though capitalism may continue to exist in more advanced countries. [Italics mine, AMS.]

Here we have the fundamental postulates of Lenin's theory of the proletarian revolution. (*Leninism*, Vol. I, p. 190.)

Lenin achieves his aim of harmonizing Marxian doctrine with the idea of a proletarian revolution in Russia only by disembowelling Marxism. It is difficult to find a doctrine more central to Marx's social analysis than his theory of revolution, yet this doctrine is completely replaced by Lenin.

The opportunists in every land maintain that the proletarian revolution can begin—if it ever does begin anywhere according to their theories!—only in countries of advanced industrial development, and that the chances of a victory for socialism in such countries are increased in proportion to the extent of their industrial development. . . . Now Lenin, already during the days of the great war, basing his contention upon the law of the irregular development of imperialist States, contraposed this theory of the opportunists by his own theory of the proletarian revolution, which is: that socialism can be victorious in one country alone *even when that country is in a condition of backward capitalist development.* (*Ibid.*, p. 191.) [Italics mine.]

On the basis of the "law" of the irregular development of imperialist states, discovered by himself, Lenin revised Marx to suit his own needs.

This was a *new* and complete theory of the Socialist revolution, a theory affirming the possibility of the victory of Socialism in separate countries, and indicating the conditions of this victory and its prospects . . .

This theory fundamentally differed from the view current among the Marxists in the period of *pre-imperialist* capitalism. . . . On the basis of the facts concerning *imperialist* capitalism set forth in his remarkable book, *Imperialism, The Highest Stage of Capitalism*, Lenin displaced this view as obsolete and set forth a new theory . . . (*History of the C.P.S.U.*, pp. 169-170.)

As a result of a study of imperialist capitalism, Lenin, on the basis of the Marxist theory, arrived at the conclusion that the old formula of Engels and Marx no longer corresponded to the new historical conditions, and that the victory of the Socialist revolution was quite possible in one country, taken singly. The opportunists of all countries clung to the old formula of

Engels and Marx and accused Lenin of departing from
Marxism. But it was Lenin, of course, who was the
real Marxist who had mastered the theory of Marxism,
and not the opportunists, for Lenin was advancing the
Marxist theory by enriching it with new experience,
whereas the opportunists were dragging it back, mum-
mifying it. (*Ibid.*, p. 357.)

Since Lenin continues to use the Marxian concept of class
his theory of revolution is at bottom as fallacious as Marx's.
The principal advantage that it has over Marx's theory is that
it is completely lacking in precision. Marx stated that the
proletarian revolutions would occur in those countries which
were industrially most advanced. Yet in neither England,
France, Germany, nor the United States have proletarian revolutions occurred. Lenin and Stalin do not go out on a limb in
any such fashion. The revolution will next occur, they say,
wherever the world front of imperialism is most vulnerable.
Where is this most vulnerable spot? That can only be known
after the fact. That can only be known *after* the revolution
has taken place.

In 1917 . . . Russia was the weakest part of the imperialist world-front, although in Russia capitalism
was so much less developed than in France, Germany,
Great Britain, or the United States of America.

Where is the front likely to be broken next? Again
at the weakest point, obviously. Perhaps that will be in
British India, where there is a young and combative
revolutionary proletariat, allied to the champions of
the movement for national liberation—a movement
which is certainly very powerful. In India, moreover,
the anti-revolutionary forces are incorporated in a foreign imperialism, which has completely forfeited moral
credit and has incurred the general hatred of the oppressed and exploited masses.

Another possibility is that the next breach in the
imperialist world-front will occur in Germany. The

factors at work in India are beginning to operate in Germany as well. (*Leninism*, Vol. I, pp. 101-102.)

The revolution can occur with equal ease in countries as unlike as India and Germany. No matter where a "proletarian revolution" occurs, Stalin can explain it by saying that it was there that the world front of imperialism was weakest.

A second difficulty had to be overcome before the October Revolution could be presented as the proletarian revolution forecast by Marxian theory. According to Marx, society changes from a feudal to an industrial condition during the interval between the bourgeois and proletarian revolutions. The bourgeoisie develops its powers and finally decays, while the proletariat is born and comes to maturity. England had its bourgeois revolution in 1688, according to Marx, and France had its bourgeois revolution in 1789. By 1917, 229 years had elapsed in the one case, and 128 in the other, without either of these nations having yet had its "proletarian revolution." In Russia, however, the proletarian revolution was supposed to follow the bourgeois revolution of February 1917 by a matter of months.

This could appear credible only if the pace of revolution were regarded as enormously accelerated during these few months. It is precisely this assumption of acceleration that Lenin and Stalin are forced to make.

> These eight months of revolutionary crisis must be regarded as equivalent to at least eight years of normal constitutional development . . . (*Leninism*, Vol. I, p. 221.)

Lenin speaks of the World War as a "mighty accelerator," (*Essentials of Lenin*, Vol. I, p. 752) and states that the "imperialist war" has "so accelerated the course of development of backward Russia that we have 'at a single stroke,' (or rather as *it seemed at a single stroke*) caught up with Italy, England, and almost with France . . ." (*Ibid.*, p. 755.)

Since "classes," as Marx conceived them, have never existed, it follows that whatever the October events may have represented, they did not represent the overthrow of one class by another. The disparity between the Leninist-Stalinist version of the October revolution and the picture of it presented by careful historical accounts measures, I believe, the gulf between the ideal and the reality. On close examination, the mighty "proletarian revolution" appears to have been nothing more than a *coup d'état*. Instead of the great mass uprising of proletarians and poor peasants of which Lenin and Stalin speak, we see the seizure of power by a small, skillfully led, band of men. This *coup d'état*, involving a comparatively few thousand men and almost deserving to be described as a palace revolution, is presented as the cataclysmic overthrow of one class and the accession to power of another. This *coup*, this seizure of power by the Bolsheviks, is presented as the proletarian revolution scientifically forecast by Marxist theory.

The actual seizure of power took place in Moscow and St. Petersburg and hinged on such things as the capture of a few important buildings and the suggestibility of a handful of soldiers. How this seizure of the state apparatus by a small group of conspirators came to be accepted as the tremendous event foretold by Marx is hard to say. The explanation is probably to be found in the faith with which rank and file Communists of that time adhered to Marxist doctrines. Marx made his prophecies on the basis of what he believed were iron historical laws. Those who believed his doctrines felt that they *knew* what the future held. There was no question in their minds but that those things which Marx had prophesied would come to pass. It was quite natural therefore that they should regard those things which did come to pass as the fulfillment of the prophecies. Blinded by Marxian theory, they saw only those things which they were prepared to see. Their faith allowed them to falsify reality to an astounding extent. When Lenin insisted that his *coup* was the uprising foretold by Marx and Engels, loyal Marxists had no difficulty in seeing it as exactly that.

So effectively has Lenin's interpretation of the October events been propagated, in fact, that a great many non-Marxists accept it as the only possible interpretation. Revolutionary changes have, of course, taken place in Russia since the October *coup*, but they have had little to do with the kind of revolution forecast by Karl Marx. They are to be explained rather by the industrialization of the country and by the imposition upon it of rigid patterns of political, social and economic behavior.

The extent to which rank-and-file members of the Communist Party were hypnotized is revealed by the great difficulty that many of them experienced in adjusting to the failure of the world revolution to occur. Marx had predicted a *world* proletarian revolution and when it failed to appear, faithful Communists were faced with a problem similar to that confronting the members of a sect organized around the belief that the world will end on a given day. What is to be done when the appointed hour arrives and doom does not descend? They must either give up their religion or find that they have made some careless error in computing the day of doom.

The world revolution failed to materialize for the simple reason that there were no forces tending to produce such a world-wide upheaval. It failed to occur because the Marxian theory of revolution is faulty from top to bottom. The February revolution was not a "bourgeois" revolution and the October *coup* was not a "proletarian revolution." These events as well as the non-appearance of the world revolution can be explained without recourse to any involved theory of the universe, history and "classes." Stalin, understandingly enough, prefers to find that Marxist theory is still intact and that the coming of the world revolution has only been postponed.

What do we mean when we say that the revolution has suffered a set-back, has entered a period of calm? Is not this the beginning of the end of the world revolution, the liquidation of the proletarian revolution throughout the world? Lenin told us that, once the proletariat had triumphed in our own land, a new epoch would begin, the epoch of the world revolution, an epoch full of conflicts and wars, of flow and ebb, of victories and defeats, an epoch which would, in the end, lead to the victory of the proletariat in the chief capitalist countries. But if the revolution in Europe has begun to decline, must we not conclude that Lenin's theory of a new epoch, the epoch of world revolution, is out of date? Does this not mean that the proletarian revolution in the West is no longer a question of practical politics?

Nothing of the kind!

The epoch of world revolution constitutes a new stage in the revolution, it covers a whole strategic period which may occupy years or even decades. In the course of this period there will occur, nay, must occur, ebbs and flows in the revolutionary tide. (*Leninism*, Vol. I, p. 220.)

By inventing the theory of "ebbs and flows in the revolutionary tide," and by stressing the length of the "epoch of world revolutions," Stalin lessens the embarrassment created by the failure of the world revolution to appear.

Since the October victory we have been living in the third strategic period, the third stage of the revolution, during which our objective is the overthrow of the international bourgeoisie. It is difficult to foresee how long this period will last. Certainly it will cover a goodly span of time, and we shall witness a succession of ebbs and flows in the revolutionary tide. (*Leninism*, Vol. I, p. 222.)

By stating that the present stage of development must cover a "goodly span of time" Stalin moves the date for the revolution an indefinite distance into the future and thus dismisses it in the same fashion that the problem of the withering away of the state was dismissed.

It was part of Lenin's theory of revolution that the Communists would enjoy the support of the industrial laborers and the poor peasants. This support is, therefore, assumed to have existed.

> In the first place, the October revolution could count upon the support of the most active majority of the workers throughout Russia.
>
> Secondly, it could count on the support of the poorer peasants and that of the war-weary and land-hungry soldiers. (*Leninism*, Vol. I, p. 182.)

Waiving the question of the extent to which the Bolshevik seizure of power enjoyed the support of Russia's then small group of industrial laborers, it can be said with certainty that peasant participation and support of the seizure was all but non-existent. The lack of peasant enthusiasm for Bolshevik rule is made evident by the fact that it took the "proletarian revolution" a year to "spread" to remote rural districts. (*Essentials of Lenin*, Vol. II, p. 417.) In other words, a year elapsed before the Bolsheviks were able to overcome all open resistance to their seizure of power. The way in which this proletarian revolution spread is clear. The Party sent armed detachments into the country to crush all resistance to Bolshevik rule.

> The Soviet Republic sends into the rural districts detachments of armed workers, primarily the most advanced, from the capitals. These workers carry Socialism into the countryside, win over the poor, organize and enlighten them, and help them to *suppress the resistance of the bourgeoisie.* (*Ibid.*, p. 416.)

Lenin states that these armed bands help the peasants suppress the bourgeoisie, but he does not say how a bourgeois is to be recognized. He does not say that these bands punish those whom they *suspect* of being bourgeois, but that they punish those who *are* bourgeois. This way of thinking calls to mind a passage in which Stalin speaks of the secret police.

The G.P.U., or the Cheka, is a punitive organ of the Soviet government. It is more or less similar to the Committee of Public Safety which existed during the great French Revolution. It punishes primarily spies, plotters, terrorists, bandits, speculators and forgers. It is something in the nature of a military political tribunal set up for the purpose of protecting the interests of the Revolution from attacks on the part of the counter-revolutionary bourgeoisie and their agents.

This organ was created on the day after the October Revolution, after all kinds of plots, terrorist and spying organisations, financed by Russian and foreign capitalists were discovered. This organ developed and became consolidated after a series of terrorist acts had been perpetrated against the leaders of the Soviet Government. . . . It must be admitted that the G.P.U. aimed at the enemies of the revolution without missing. . . . It has been, ever since, the terror of the bourgeoisie, the indefatigable guard of the Revolution, the unsheathed sword of the proletariat.

It is not surprising, therefore, that the bourgeoisie of all countries hate the G.P.U. All sorts of legends have been invented about the G.P.U. The slander that has been circulated about the G.P.U. knows no bounds. And what does that mean? It means that the G.P.U. is properly defending the interests of the Revolution. The sworn enemies of the Revolution curse the G.P.U. Hence it follows that the G.P.U. is doing the right thing.

But this is not how the workers regard the G.P.U. You go to the workers' districts and ask the workers what they think of it. You will find that they regard it with great respect. Why? Because they see in it a loyal defender of the Revolution.

I understand the hatred and distrust of the bourgeoisie for the G.P.U. . . . But I cannot understand some workers' delegates who, on coming to the U.S.S.R., ask with alarm as to whether many counter-revolutionaries have been punished by the G.P.U. and whether terrorists and plotters against the proletarian Government will still be punished by it and is it not time yet for its dissolution. Where does this concern of some workers' delegates for the enemies of the proletarian revolution come from? How can it be explained? How can it be justified?

They advocate a maximum of leniency, they advise the dissolution of the G.P.U. . . . But can anyone guarantee that the capitalists of all countries will abandon the idea of organising and financing counter-revolutionary plotters, terrorists, incendiaries, and bomb-throwers after the liquidation of the G.P.U.? To disarm the Revolution without any guarantees that the enemies of the Revolution will be disarmed—would not that be folly, would not that be a crime against the working class? (*Leninism*, Vol. II, pp. 97-98.)

It is taken for granted that those whom the G.P.U. punishes are, in fact, enemies of the proletariat. It is said, for example, that the G.P.U. "aimed at the enemies of the revolution without missing." Apparently it did its job to perfection, punishing the guilty, all the guilty, and none but the guilty. Ideal retributive justice is assumed to have been achieved in practice. By virtue of the assumption that the actual secret police is as infallible as an ideal police, the crucial problem of how a class enemy is to be known is defined out of existence. Once it is assumed that the secret police punishes only class enemies, it follows that all those whom it has punished *were* class enemies. Reasoning moves backward from the fact of punishment to the certainty of guilt. They were punished, therefore they were guilty. This mode of thought is an important prop for the Dictator's regime since it allows his secret police organization to punish whomever it chooses while resting confident that Leninist theory will support the contention that all the victims were indeed guilty. Just as it is assumed that the secret police has infallible means for knowing the enemies of the working class, so it is assumed that the armed bands sent by the Party into the rural districts knew who were bourgeois.

The problem of how class enemies are to be recognized is overlooked, not accidentally, but in accord with settled policy. The entire "dictatorship of the proletariat" is *defined* as the suppression of the bourgeoisie, but nowhere are instructions given for recognizing these class enemies.

> The dictatorship of the proletariat is a revolutionary authority forcibly imposed upon the bourgeoisie . . . is the dictatorship of the exploited majority over the exploiting minority.

> To put it briefly, *the dictatorship of the proletariat is the rule of the proletariat over the bourgeoisie, a rule unrestricted by law, based upon force, enjoying the sympathy and the support of the labouring and exploited masses.* (*Leninism*, Vol. I, pp. 114-115.)

> The revolutionary dictatorship of the proletariat is rule won and maintained by the use of violence by the proletariat against the bourgeoisie, rule that is unrestricted by any laws. (*Essentials of Lenin*, Vol. II, p. 365.)

> The necessary earmark, the essential condition of dictatorship, is the *forcible* suppression of the exploiters as a *class* . . . (*Ibid.*, p. 380.)

Since there is no "bourgeoisie," in the Marxian sense of that term, who are the persons being suppressed in the name of the suppression of the bourgeoisie? In practice the term comes to refer to anyone, regardless of occupation or relation to the means of production, who is hostile or is suspected of being hostile to the Party. Instead of accepting the Stalinist contention that those persons who are punished *are* bourgeoisie, it must be said that those persons who are punished *become* bourgeoisie.

Precisely the same situation exists in connection with the "Kulaks."

To attack the kulaks means to smash the kulaks, to liquidate them as a class. Without these aims, attack is a declamation, mere scratching, empty noise, anything but a real Bolshevist attack. To attack the kulaks means to make proper preparations and then deliver the blow, a blow from which they could not recover. That is what we Bolsheviks call a real attack. (*Leninism*, Vol. II, p. 270.)

What does that mean? It means that we have gone over from a policy of restricting the exploiting tendencies of the kulaks to the policy of *liquidating* the kulaks as a class. (*Ibid.*, p. 271.)

We have tolerated these bloodsuckers, spiders, and vampires, pursuing a policy of restricting their exploiting tendencies. . . . There is no longer any reason to tolerate these spiders and bloodsuckers . . . who are burning down collective farms, murdering the advocates of collective farming, and attempting to undermine the sowing campaign, [to tolerate them] any longer would be to go against the interests of the workers and peasants. (*Ibid.*, p. 304.)

It is clear that an attack is about to be directed against persons Stalin is calling "kulaks." Except for a number of general statements to the effect that they are bloodsuckers, spiders and vampires, little is said to distinguish a kulak from a non-kulak. Whereas in some countries a great effort is made to define precisely who is and who is not within a category affected by legislation, here the tacit assumption is that everyone knows what a kulak is and that there is, therefore, no need for definition. The result is that all opposition to the Party and its agricultural programs can be liquidated in the name of the liquidation of the kulaks.

The same sort of ambiguity is to be found in connection with such terms as "worker" and "proletarian."

Kautsky does not understand this truth, which is so obvious and intelligible to every worker . . . (*Essentials of Lenin*, Vol. II, p. 375.)

And this simple truth, a truth that is as plain as noonday to every class-conscious worker (representing the masses, and not an upper stratum of petty-bourgeois scoundrels who have been bribed by the capitalists, such as are the social-imperialists of all countries), this truth, which is obvious to every representative of the exploited classes . . . (*Ibid.*, p. 365.)

By saying that certain "truths" are obvious to every worker and every true representative of the working class, Lenin implies that those who do not perceive these truths cannot be workers. It is not sufficient that a man work, say, as a laborer in a factory, in order to qualify as a "worker." To be accepted as a "worker" by Lenin and Stalin an individual must satisfy certain conditions that concern not his occupation but his beliefs.

This chapter has been devoted to distinguishing certain realities from their ideal descriptions. When Communists speak of the "October Revolution" as having brought the proletariat to power, for example, it must be understood that what is involved is the *coup d'état* of October 1917 which brought the Communist Party to power. When they speak of the dictatorship of the proletariat over the bourgeoisie, it must be realized that by "proletariat" they refer to those who accept Party guidance and by "bourgeoisie" they mean all persons not actively supporting the Party. When Stalin speaks of the liquidation of the "kulaks" this must be understood to mean the liquidation of all who resist the collectivization program, not merely the rich peasants.

Continuing in the same vein, the following chapter will show the necessity of distinguishing various Soviet political and economic realities from the ideal descriptions of them found in the writings of Lenin and Stalin.

CHAPTER X

Real and Ideal: II

THE following passage is quoted from Marx's *Civil War in France.*

Wonderful, indeed, was the change the Commune had wrought in Paris! No longer any trace of the meretricious Paris of the Second Empire. No longer was Paris the rendezvous of British landlords, Irish absentees, American ex-slaveholders and shoddy men, Russian ex-serf-owners, and Wallachian boyards. No more corpses at the morgue, no nocturnal burglaries, scarcely any robberies; in fact, for the first time since the days of February, 1848, the streets of Paris were safe, and that without police of any kind. "We," said a member of the Commune, "hear no longer of assassination, theft, and personal assault; it seems, indeed, as if the police had dragged along with it to Versailles all its conservative friends." The *cocottes* had refound the scent of their protectors—the absconding men of family, religion, and, above all, of property. In their stead, the real women of Paris showed again at the surface,—heroic, noble, and devoted, like the women of antiquity. Working, thinking, fighting, bleeding Paris—almost forgetful, in its incubation of a new society, of the cannibals at its gates—radiant in the enthusiasm of its historic initiative!

Opposed to this new world at Paris, behold the old world at Versailles—that assembly of the ghouls of all defunct regimes, Legitimists and Orleanists, eager to feed upon the carcass of the nation—with a tail of antediluvian Republicans, sanctioning, by their presence in the Assembly, the slave holders' rebellion, relying for their maintenance of their Parliamentary Republic upon the vanity of the senile mountebank at its head, and caricaturing 1789 by holding their ghastly meetings in the *Jeu de Paume*. There it was, this Assembly, the representative of everything dead in France, propped up into a semblance of life by nothing but the swords of the generals of Louis Bonaparte. Paris all truth, Versailles all lies . . . (*Civil War in France*, p. 414.)

Paris of the Commune is all that is good, radiant, noble, new and true. Versailles, the symbol of the old society, represents all that is dead, corrupt, and decaying. Paris of the Commune, "working, thinking, fighting, bleeding Paris" is "radiant" and its women are "heroic, noble and devoted." The government at Versailles is composed of "ghouls" "propped into a semblance of life," holding its "ghastly" meetings. Its soldiers are "cannibals," its women *cocottes*.

The contrast is that between the incarnation of perfection and the incarnation of evil and corruption. "Paris all truth, Versailles all lies. . . ." Paris is incubating the society of the future, while Versailles represents "everything dead in France." "The direct antithesis to the Empire was the Commune." (*Civil War in France*, p. 403.) To Paris of the Commune, Marx imputes all the virtues of his ideal city, a romanticized Greek *polis*. To Versailles, on the other hand, he imputes all the characteristics of a bestial, decadent, exploiting society. In neither case is a distinction made between the reality and the ideal.

The same drawing in black and white, the same free imputation of ideal characteristics to a reality, is found in the writings of Lenin and Stalin. Soviet society is held to possess all the virtues that an ideal communistic society ought to possess, while "bourgeois" nations are assumed to have all the undesirable characteristics that Marxist theory attributes to them. This chapter will show the extreme terms in which life in the U.S.S.R. has been described by Lenin and Stalin and will indicate the gulf separating this ideal picture from reality. First, several aspects of the Soviet Union's social and political life will be dealt with: the classless society; its "democratic" elections; freedom of press and assembly. The same identification of ideal and reality will then be shown to exist in the economic realm.

In 1936 Stalin decreed that class conflicts had become a thing of the past in the Soviet Union. From that time on, Communist writings presented Soviet society as the realization of the ideal classless society of Marxist theory. The same complete harmony of interests that Marx and Engels assumed to exist among the members of a "class" has been extended to all the inhabitants of an enormous geographical area.

> The feature that distinguishes Soviet society today from any capitalist society is that it no longer contains antagonistic, hostile classes; that the exploiting classes have been eliminated, while the workers, peasants and intellectuals, who make up Soviet society, live and work in friendly collaboration. While capitalist society is torn by irreconcilable contradictions between workers and capitalists and between peasants and landlords—resulting in its internal instability—Soviet society, liberated from the yoke of exploitation, knows no such contradictions, is free of class conflicts, and presents a picture of friendly collaboration between workers, peasants and intellectuals. (*From Socialism to Communism in the Soviet Union*, p. 35.)

Internal difficulties are no longer explained as arising out of desperate acts committed by the remaining capitalist elements, but instead are explained as the works of spies and saboteurs hired by capitalist powers. This assumed absence of groups with conflicting interests is, of course, used to justify the monopoly of legality held by the Party. Since the bourgeoisie has been liquidated and only proletarians remain in the Soviet Union, there is need for but a single proletarian party, the Communist Party.

In the past, the conflict of opinion among the workers and the toiling peasantry was concentrated mainly on questions concerning the overthrow of the landlords, of tsarism, of the bourgeoisie, and of the break-up of the whole capitalist system. Now, however, under the dictatorship of the proletariat, conflict of opinion does not revolve around questions concerning the overthrow of the Soviet Government, of the break-up of the Soviet system, but around questions concerning the improvement of the organs of the Soviet Government and the improvement of their work. This makes a radical difference.

There is nothing surprising in the fact that the conflict of opinion in the past around questions concerning the revolutionary destruction of the prevailing system gave grounds for the appearance of several rival parties in the working class and toiling masses of the peasantry. . . . On the other hand, it is not difficult to understand that conflict of opinion under the dictatorship of the proletariat, which has for its aim not the break-up of the existing Soviet system, but its improvement and consolidation, provides no nourishment for the existence of several Parties among the workers and the toiling masses in the rural districts. That is why the legality of a single Party, the Communist Party, the monopoly enjoyed by that Party, not only raises no objection among the workers and toiling peasants but, on the contrary, is accepted by them as something necessary and desirable. (*Leninism*, Vol. II, pp. 57-58.)

Under this one-party regime real democracy has for the first time been achieved.

For the first time in history Soviet or proletarian democracy created *democracy* for the masses, for the toilers, for the workers and small peasants.

Never before in history has there been a state representing the majority of the population, the *actual* rule of the majority, such as is the Soviet state. (*Essentials of Lenin*, Vol. II, p. 476.)

Proletarian democracy is a million times more democratic than any bourgeois democracy; Soviet power is a million times more democratic than the most democratic bourgeois republic. (*Ibid.*, p. 374.)

Political life in the Soviet Union has been "completely democratized" according to Stalin (*From Socialism to Communism in the Soviet Union*, p. 19) and the democratic nature of Soviet elections is merely one expression of this democratization.

Never in the history of the world have there been such really free and really democratic elections—never! History knows no other example like it. [Applause] The point is not that our elections will be universal, equal, secret and direct, although that fact in itself is of great importance. The point is that our universal elections will be carried out as the freest elections and the most democratic of any country in the world.

Universal elections exist and are held in some capitalist countries, too, so-called democratic countries. But in what atmosphere are elections held there? In an atmosphere of class conflicts, in an atmosphere of class enmity, in an atmosphere of pressure brought to bear on the electors by the capitalists, landlords, bankers, and other capitalist sharks. Such elections, even if they are universal, equal, secret, and direct, cannot be called altogether free and altogether democratic elections.

Here, in our country, on the contrary, elections are held in an entirely different atmosphere. Here there are no capitalists and no landlords and, consequently, no pressure is exerted by propertied classes on non-propertied class. Here elections are held in an atmosphere of collaboration between the workers, the peasants and the intelligentsia, in an atmosphere of mutual confidence between them, in an atmosphere, I would say, of mutual friendship; because there are no capitalists in our country, no landlords, no exploitation and nobody, in fact, to bring pressure to bear on the people in order to distort their will. (Stalin, quoted in *Essentials of Lenin*, Vol. I, p. 46.)

One of the notable things about these "only really free and really democratic elections in the whole world" is that they never fail to record an overwhelming majority for the Communist Party ticket.

As to the elections themselves, they were a magnificent demonstration of that unity of Soviet society and of that amity among the nations of the U.S.S.R. which constitute the characteristic feature of the internal situation of our country. As we know, in the elections to the Supreme Soviet of the U.S.S.R. in December 1937, nearly ninety million votes, or 98.6 per cent of the total vote, were cast for the Communist and non-Party bloc, while in the elections to the Supreme Soviets of the Union Republics in June 1938, ninety-two million votes, or 99.4 per cent of the total vote, were cast for the Communist and non-Party bloc. (*From Socialism to Communism in the Soviet Union*, p. 36.)

To suggestions that purges of former Party leaders had reduced support for the Party, Stalin replies that this obviously is not the case since after each new batch of executions the Party's vote increased.

Certain foreign newspaper writers have been talking drivel to the effect that the purging of the Soviet organizations of spies, assassins, and wreckers like Trotsky, Zinoviev, Kamenev, Yakir, Tukhachevsky, Rosengoltz, Bukharin and other fiends has "shaken" the Soviet system and caused its "demoralization." One can only laugh at such cheap drivel. How can the purging of Soviet organizations of noxious and hostile elements shake and demoralize the Soviet system? This Trotsky-Bukharin bunch of spies, murderers and wreckers, who kowtowed to the foreign world, who were possessed by a slavish instinct to grovel before every foreign bigwig, and who were ready to enter his employ as spies . . . who needs this miserable band of venal slaves, of what value can they be to the people, and whom can they "demoralize"? In 1937 Tukhachevsky, Yakir, Uborevich and other fiends were sentenced to be shot. After that, the elections to the Supreme Soviet of the U.S.S.R. were held. In these elections 98.6 per cent of the total vote was cast for the Soviet power. At the beginning of 1938 Rosengoltz, Rykov, Bukharin and other fiends were sentenced to be shot. After that, the elections to the Supreme Soviets of the Union Republics were held. In these elections 99.4 per cent of the total vote was cast for the Soviet power. Where are the symptoms of "demoralization," we would like to know, and why was this "demoralization" not reflected in the results of the elections? (*From Socialism to Communism in the Soviet Union*, pp. 36-37.)

In order to understand the majorities piled up by the Communist Party in these plebiscites, its position as "the only legal Party in the country," (*Leninism*, Vol. II, p. 58.) must be remembered. There are no opposition parties, no opposition candidates, and no anti-Communist ballot counters. The fiction is a country wholly united behind its representatives; the reality is a population denied any role in choosing its masters. Instead of a real choice there is only the formality of ballot casting.

Freedom of press and assembly are also among the unprecedented freedoms to be found in the democracy of the toilers.

Freedom of the press ceases to be hypocrisy, because the printing plants and stocks of paper are taken away from the bourgeoisie. The same thing applies to the best buildings, the palaces, the mansions and manor houses. The Soviet government took thousands and thousands of these best buildings from the exploiters at one stroke, and in this way made the right of assembly—without which democracy is a fraud—a million times more "democratic." (*Essentials of Lenin*, Vol. II, p. 374.)

Is there a single country in the world, even among the most democratic bourgeois countries, in which the *average rank-and-file* worker, the average rank-and-file *village laborer*, or village semi-proletarian, generally (i.e., the representative of the oppressed masses, the overwhelming majority of the population), enjoys anything approaching such *liberty* of holding meetings in the best buildings, such *liberty* to use the largest printing plants and biggest stocks of paper to express his ideas and defend his interests, such *liberty* to promote men and women of his own class, to administer and to "run" the state, as in Soviet Russia? (*Ibid.*)

Freedom of the press ceases to be hypocrisy, because the printing presses and stocks of paper are taken from the bourgeoisie. Who decides who are the bourgeoisie? Lenin made the answer clear even before the seizure of power.

State power in the shape of Soviets takes *all* the printing presses and *all* paper and distributes them *justly* . . . (Lenin, *Collected Works*, Vol. XXI, Book I, p. 175.)

Such distribution of paper and printing presses would be just, and, with power in the hands of the Soviets, would be realised without any difficulty. (*Ibid.*)

The Party is to take over the printing presses and distribute them "justly," i.e., as it sees fit. Only proletarian newspapers, that is Communist Party organs, are to be allowed an existence. The following is the freedom of the press that emerges:

Dear comrades:

I protest decidedly against the publication in *Proletarskaya Revolyutsia* (No. 6, 1930) of Slutski's anti-Party and semi-Trotskian article, "The Bolsheviks on German Social-Democracy in the Period of its Pre-War Crisis," as a discussion article.

. . . And you, instead of branding this newfound "historian" as a slanderer and falsifier, enter into discussion with him, give him a platform. I cannot refrain from protesting against the publication of Slutski's article in your journal as a discussion article, since the question of Lenin's Bolshevism, the question as to whether Lenin *did or did not* carry on an unrelenting struggle against centrism as a certain form of opportunism, the question as to whether Lenin *was* or *was not* a real Bolshevik cannot be converted into a subject of discussion.

In your statement sent "in the name of the editors" to the Central Committee on October 20, you acknowledge that the editors made a mistake in publishing Slutski's article as a discussion article. That is, of course, a good thing, despite the fact that the editors' statement was very belated. But in your statement you commit a fresh mistake when you declare that "the editors consider it to be politically extremely urgent and necessary that the entire complex of problems connected with the mutual relations between the Bolsheviks and the pre-war Second International be further discussed in the pages of *Proletarskaya Revolyutsia*. That means that you intend again to draw people into discussion on questions which represent the axioms of Bolshevism. . . . But you are attempting to drag us backward by turning an axiom into a problem requiring "further discussion"! Why? On what ground? . . . (*Leninism*, Vol. II, pp. 446-47.)

Slutski asserts that so far a sufficient quantity of official documents has not been found to prove Lenin's (The Bolshevik's) determined and relentless struggle against centrism. He employs that bureaucratic thesis as an irrefutable argument in favour of the postulate that Lenin (the Bolsheviks) underestimated the danger of centrism in the Second International. And you set about arguing against this nonsense, against this rascally hairsplitting. But what is there, properly speaking, to argue about? Is it not plain, without arguing, that by his talk about documents Slutski is trying to cover up the wretchedness and falsity of his so-called position? (*Ibid.*, p. 454.)

You yourselves understand that it is not the business of the editors to facilitate the smuggling activity of such "historians" by granting them the platform for discussion.

* * *

With comradely greetings
J. Stalin
(*Ibid.*, p. 458.)

There is freedom of the press so long as the editors of newspapers and journals take care to publish only material acceptable to Party leadership. The fiction is an unparalleled freedom of the press, the reality is a control of the press seldom if ever equalled.

An interesting point is the way in which the class analysis is used by Lenin and Stalin to hollow out conceptions like those of freedom of press and of assembly.

"The right of assembly" may be taken as an example of the demands of "pure democracy." Every class conscious worker who has not broken connections with his class will understand at once that it would be absurd to promise the right of assembly to the exploiters in the period and in the circumstances in which the exploiters are resisting their overthrow and are defending their privileges. (Lenin, *Selected Works*, Vol. VII, pp. 225-226.)

Once it is accepted that there are two "classes" locked in a life and death struggle, anything done by one "class" to the other can be justified in the name of survival. The crushing of the "bourgeoisie" by force is made a condition for the freeing of humanity.

We must crush them [the capitalists, the oppressors] in order to free humanity from wage-slavery; their resistance must be broken by force; it is clear that where there is suppression, where there is coercion, there is no freedom and no democracy. (*Essentials of Lenin*, Vol. II, p. 201.)

That which is good for one class is ipso facto bad for the other. One class can be free only if it denies freedom to the other.

Hence, so long as there are exploiters who rule the majority, the exploited, the democratic state must inevitably be a democracy for the exploiters. A state of the exploited must fundamentally differ from such a state; it must be a democracy for the exploited, and a means of *suppressing the exploiters;* and the suppression of a class means inequality for that class, its exclusion from "democracy." (*Essentials of Lenin*, Vol. II, p. 376.)

There can be no talk of freedom or democracy in general but only of freedom for one class and suppression of the other. "A liberal naturally speaks of 'democracy' in general; but a Marxist will never forget to ask, 'for what class?'" (*Essentials of Lenin*, Vol. II, p. 364.)

After the seizure of power Lenin, rightly gauging that the socialists were the Bolsheviks' most serious ideological competitors, quickly termed a great many of their newspapers "bourgeois" and "counter-revolutionary" and had them suppressed. He answered the protests of the Mensheviks and Socialist-Revolutionaries by turning one of their favorite arguments against them. He mocked them by pointing out that only recently they had been vociferous in their insistence that there was no such thing as "democracy in general" and that it all depended on which "class" exercised the dictatorship.

> In their books and pamphlets, in the resolutions of their congresses and in their agitational speeches, the Socialists of all countries have explained to the people the class character of these bourgeois revolutions, of this bourgeois dictatorship, a thousand and a million times. Hence, the present defence of bourgeois democracy cloaked in speeches about "democracy in general" and the present howling and shouting against the dictatorship of the proletariat cloaked by cries about a "dictatorship in general" are a downright betrayal of socialism, the practical desertion to the side of the bourgeoisie . . . (Lenin, *Selected Works*, Vol. VII, p. 224.)

By their failure to perceive that Marxian classes were fictions and that the decision as to who was and who was not a "bourgeois" could, therefore, be very arbitrary, these socialists accepted a doctrine that was with ease turned against them.

According to the claims thus far examined in this chapter, classes have been abolished in the Soviet Union, elections there are a "million times" more democratic than in any western country, democracy for the poor has for the first time been established, and the toiling masses possess unexampled freedom of press and assembly. This headlong identification of the Soviet reality with the Marxian ideal does not stop with the political sphere, but extends to the economic as well.

For example, the rule of the exploiters has been ended, and the common man now gives the orders.

That is why the October Revolution commenced this systematic and unswerving struggle to compel the exploiters to cease their resistance and become reconciled to the thought . . . that the rule of the exploiting classes has been abolished forever, that from now on the simple muzhik will give the orders and that they must obey, however unpleasant that may be. (Lenin, *Selected Works*, Vol. VII, p. 269.)

The exploitation of man by man has been eradicated, precisely as Marx said it would be.

The victory of Socialism in all branches of the national economy had abolished the exploitation of man by man. (*History of the C.P.S.U.* p. 319.)

The sum and substance of the achievements of the First Five-Year Plan was that they had completely emancipated the workers and peasants from exploitation and had opened the way to a prosperous and cultured life for ALL working people in the U.S.S.R. (*Ibid.*, p. 320.)

The liquidation of parasitic classes has led to the disappearance of the exploitation of man by man. The labour of the worker and peasant is freed from exploitation. (*Socialism Victorious*, p. 48.)

The peasants, freed from exploitation, are happily located on collective farms.

Now an entirely new peasantry had grown up in the U.S.S.R. There were no longer any landlords, kulaks, merchants and usurers to exploit the peasants. The overwhelming majority of the peasant households had joined the collective farms, which were based not on private ownership, but on collective ownership of the means of production, collective ownership which had grown from collective labour. This was a new type of peasantry, a peasantry emancipated from all exploitation. (*History of the C.P.S.U.*, pp. 343-344.)

The lot of the worker has improved as much as that of the peasant. Labor has even ceased to be a burden.

> The most remarkable feature of competition is the radical revolution it has wrought in men's views of labour, because it transforms labour from a disgraceful and painful burden, as it was reckoned before, into a matter of *honour*, a matter of *glory*, a matter of *valour and heroism*. There is not, and cannot be, anything similar to it in capitalist countries. There, under the capitalists, the most desirable end which earns social approval is to have an income, to live on one's property, and to be free from toil which is regarded as a contemptible occupation. Here in our U.S.S.R. on the contrary, the most desirable course which earns social approval, becomes the possibility of being a hero of labour, a hero of the shock brigade movement surrounded with the glamour of the respect of millions of toilers. (*Leninism*, Vol. II, p. 365.)

All economic ills have been eradicated.

> In the U.S.S.R. there are no strikes and a *growth* of labour enthusiasm among the workers and peasants which *gives* our social system millions of additional working days. (*Ibid.*, p. 363.)

> In the new, Socialist society, crises, poverty, unemployment and destitution had disappeared forever. The conditions had been created for a prosperous and cultured life for all members of Soviet society. (*History of the C.P.S.U.*, p. 343.)

Public ownership of productive facilities is general.

> Public, Socialist ownership of the means of production had been firmly established as the unshakable foundation of the new, Socialist system in all branches of economic life. (*History of the C.P.S.U.*, p. 343.)

Here is the ideal, the fiction. What is the reality? What, for example, is the significance of "public ownership" of the means of production? What does it mean to say that the land and factories belong to the "whole of the people"?

> Workers and peasants, toilers and exploited! The land, the banks, the factories and works now belong to the whole of the people! (*Essentials of Lenin*, Vol. II, p. 259.)

What is "ownership" when it is shared by several hundred million people, strangers to one another, spread across a continent?

What is the Soviet system of economy?

The Soviet system of economy means that:

1. The power of the capitalist class has been overthrown and has been replaced by the power of the working class.
2. The tools and means of production, the land, factories, works, etc. have been taken away from the capitalists and handed over to the working class and to the peasantry . . .
6. The working class is the master of the country, working not for the capitalists, but for its own class. (*Leninism*, Vol. II, p. 368.)

When "ownership" becomes collective it becomes unimportant. The primary concern then becomes that of control. It means little to say that the "working class" "owns" the means of production if the state controls the factories, decides what they shall produce, what prices shall be asked and so on. By focusing attention on ownership rather than on the question of control and whether or not it is democratically organized, Lenin and Stalin draw a red herring across the path.

Stalin attributes the absence of strikes in the Soviet Union to the immense enthusiasm of the Soviet workers. Article 130 of the 1936 Constitution, however, states that it is the duty of every citizen of the U.S.S.R. to "maintain labour discipline." This emphasis on "labour discipline" has been a favorite refrain of both Lenin and Stalin.

The Young Communist League must train every-
body to conscious and disciplined labour while they are
still young, from the age of twelve. (*Essentials of
Lenin*, Vol. II, p. 673.)

The stress laid on labor discipline suggests that the real
reason for the absence of strikes in the Soviet Union is the
pressure brought to bear on the workers. The position occupied by the trade unions, presumably the leaders of any strike,
bears out this supposition.

From all the foregoing it is evident that there are
a number of contradictions in the various functions of
the trade unions. On the one hand, the trade union's
principal method of operation is that of persuasion
and education; on the other hand, as participants in
the exercise of state power, they cannot refuse to participate in the work of coercion. On the one hand their
main function is to protect the interests of the masses
of the working people in the most direct and immediate sense of the term; on the other hand, as participants in the exercise of state power and builders of
the national economy as a whole, they cannot refuse
to exercise pressure. (*Essentials of Lenin*, Vol. II, p.
767.)

There are no strikes because the unions "as participants in
the exercise of state power . . . cannot refuse to exercise pressure" on their members on the orders of the Party. If unions
are denied their traditional role, do they then participate in
the management of factories?

After the proletariat has captured political power,
its principal and fundamental interests demand that
the output of manufactured goods and the productive
forces of society should be increased to enormous di-
mensions. . . To achieve this success in Russia in its
present state, it is absolutely essential that all authority in the factories should be concentrated in the hands
of the management. The factory management, usually

built up on the principle of one-man management, must have authority independently to fix wages and distribute money wages, rations, special working clothes, and all other supplies, on the basis and within the limits of collective agreements concluded with the trade unions: it must have the utmost freedom to distribute these supplies at its own discretion, to enquire strictly into the actual successes achieved in increasing output, reducing losses and increasing profits, to choose very carefully outstanding and capable managers, etc. (*Essentials of Lenin*, Vol. II, pp. 763-764.)

"Under these circumstances," Lenin concludes, "all direct interference by the trade unions in the management of factories must be regarded as positively harmful and impermissible." (*Essentials of Lenin*, Vol. II, p. 764.) Where, then, is the "simple muzhik" who was to have given the orders?

In regard to the second question concerning the significance of precisely individual dictatorial powers from the point of view of the specific tasks of the present moment, it must be said that large scale machinery and industry—which is precisely the material productive source and foundation of socialism—calls for absolute and strict unity of will, which directs the joint labours of hundreds, thousands and tens of thousands of people. The technical, economic and historical necessity of this is obvious, and all those who have thought about socialism have always regarded it as one of the conditions of socialism. But how can strict unity of will be ensured? By thousands subordinating their will to the will of one.

Given ideal class consciousness and discipline on the part of those taking part in the common work, this subordination would more than anything remind one of the mild leadership of a conductor of an orchestra. It may assume the sharp forms of a dictatorship if ideal discipline and class consciousness are lacking. But be that as it may, *unquestioning submission* to a single will is absolutely necessary for the success of labour processes that are based on large-scale machine industry. (*Selected Works*, Vol. VII, p. 342.)

The revolution has only just broken the oldest, most durable and heaviest fetters to which the masses were compelled to submit. That was yesterday. But today the same revolution demands, in the interests of socialism, that the masses *unquestioningly obey* the single will of the leaders of the labour process. (*Ibid.*, p. 342.)

The exploitation of man by man is said to have been forever abolished in the Soviet Union. What is the reality? Exploitation has not been ended, but has rather been institutionalized on an unprecedented scale.

The task of the penal policy of the proletariat during the transition from capitalism to socialism is the defense of the dictatorship of the proletariat and socialist construction being carried out by it against the encroachments of class-hostile elements and infringements, not only on the part of class elements but also of unstable elements among the workers. (Regulations governing forced labor camps in the U.S.S.R., presented by the British government to the Economic and Social Council of the United Nations, as reported in *The New York Times*, July 24, 1949, IV:3.)

The task of the penal policy of the Soviet Union is the punishment of all "class-hostile elements" and all "unstable elements" among the workers, that is, the punishment of all persons hesitant about accepting total control of their lives. Do the millions of persons in the labor colonies find labor a matter of "honor" and "glory"?

This chapter and the one preceding it have shown how Lenin and Stalin have systematically falsified the Soviet reality by attributing to it all the characteristics of an ideal socialist society. Though every attempt be made to prevent the outside world from distinguishing fact and fiction, the reality may nevertheless be glimpsed. Purges, the frantic insistence that complete unity has been achieved, the activity of the secret police, labor camps, attempts to cut the Russian people off from the outside world, the steadily swelling army of refugees from behind the Iron Curtain and their accounts of life under Communist rule—all these testify to the gap between the reality and the Communist depiction of it.

CHAPTER XI

Leviathan

LENIN never made Marx's mistake of assuming that all power could be reduced to economic power. In agitating for the October putsch, for example, he dressed up his analysis in class terms but his primary interest centered around questions of political and military power. He was intent on propagandizing the army, learning where the troops were located, seizing the telephone exchange, and so on.

The victory of the uprising is now secure for the Bolsheviks: (1) we can (if we do not "await" the Soviet Congress) launch a *sudden* attack from three points, from Petrograd, from Moscow, from the Baltic fleet; (2) we have slogans whose support is guaranteed: down with the government that suppresses the uprising of the peasants against the landowners! (3) we have a majority *in the country;* (4) complete disorganisation of the Mensheviks and S-R's: (5) we are technically in a position to seize power in Moscow (which might even be the one to start, so as to deal the enemy a surprise blow); (6) we have *thousands* of armed workers and soldiers in Petrograd who can seize *at once* the Winter Palace, the General Staff Building, the telephone exchange and all the largest printing establishments. They will not be able to drive us out from there, whereas there will be such propaganda *in the army* that it will be *impossible* to fight against this government of peace, of land for the peasants, etc. (Lenin, *Collected Works*, Vol. XXI, Book I, pp. 277-78.)

As a student of history, Lenin had an excellent grasp of the possibilities of minority revolution. As early as 1902 he wrote "Give us an organization of revolutionaries, and we shall overturn the whole of Russia! ("What Is To Be Done," in *Essentials of Lenin*, Vol. I, p. 236.) His view never changed. In August 1917 he wrote the article, "On Constitutional Illusions" from which the following passage is taken:

Beginning with the Peasant War in the Middle Ages in Germany, through all the large-scale revolutionary movements and epochs up to 1848 and 1871, and further up to 1905, we see innumerable examples of how the more organised, more class-conscious, better armed minority forces its will upon the majority and is victorious over it. (Lenin, *Collected Works*, Vol. XXI, Book I, pp. 68-69.)

Understanding how an organized minority could be victorious over a majority, Lenin had no patience with the desire of his fellow Bolsheviks to wait for some problematic event to sweep the Kerensky government out of power.

History has made the *military* question now the fundamental *political* question. I am afraid that the Bolsheviks forget this, being steeped in "day to day events," in petty current questions, and "*hoping*" that "the wave will sweep Kerensky away." Such hope is naive; it is the same as relying on chance. (*Ibid.*, p. 265.)

The comrades were too much imbued with the Marxian idea of an inevitable revolution to be brought about by the iron laws of history. It was naive, in Lenin's view, to hope for some "wave" that would sweep the Kerensky government away. The thing to do was to go out and actively seize power.

What matters is that we must make the *task* clear to the party, place on the order of the day the *armed uprising* in Petrograd and Moscow (including their regions), the conquest of power, the overthrow of the government. (Lenin, *Collected Works*, Vol. XXI, Book I, p. 222.)

Power is the thing. It must be seized. To wait is to miss the chance.

Why must the Bolsheviks assume power right now?

Because the impending surrender of Petrograd will make our chances a hundred times worse. (*Ibid.*)

It would be a disaster, or a sheer formality, to await the wavering vote of October 25. The people have the right and are in duty bound to decide such questions not by a vote, but by force . . . (*Essentials of Lenin*, Vol. II, p. 140.)

To "await" the Congress of Soviets is absolute idiocy, for this means losing *weeks*, whereas weeks and even days now decide *everything*. It means timidly to *refuse* the seizure of power . . . (Lenin, *Collected Works*, Vol. XXI, Book I, p. 277.)

If we do not do this, we may turn out to be ridiculous fools: in possession of beautiful resolutions and Soviets, but *without power!!* (*Ibid.*, p. 266.)

Lenin was preoccupied with the question of power.

Let us not forget that the question of power is the fundamental question of every revolution. (Lenin, *Collected Works*, Vol. XXI, Book I, p. 43.)

The basic question of the revolution, we said, is the question of power. (*Ibid.*, p. 46.)

This essence of the matter is that at present power can no longer be seized peacefully. (*Ibid.*, p. 45.)

The question of power can be neither evaded nor brushed aside; for this is the fundamental question which determines *everything* in the development of a revolution . . . (*Ibid.*, p. 164.)

All promises that would ease the seizure of power were made.

Only the revolutionary proletariat, only its unifying vanguard, the Bolshevik Party, can *really* carry out the

programme advanced by the poor peasants in their 242
instructions . . .

This is how we must change the line of the speeches
of workers to peasants. We workers can and will give
you what the poorest peasants want and seek . . .
(*Ibid.*, pp. 132-33.)

Trust the workers, comrade peasants . . .

. . . when in union with the city workers, in a merciless struggle against capital, you *begin* to realise the
programme of the 242 instructions, then the whole
world will come to your aid and ours; then the success
of this programme . . . will be assured. Then will
come an end to the domination of capital and to
wage-slavery. Then will begin the reign of Socialism,
the reign of peace, the reign of the toilers. (*Ibid.*, p.
134.)

The transfer of political power to the proletariat—
that is the crux of the matter. After that, everything
essential, basic, and important in the 242 instructions
will be possible of realisation. (*Ibid.*, p. 133.)

Power is the thing. After it has been seized those who
complain of broken promises can be dealt with at leisure.

The seizure of power is the business of the uprising;
its political purpose will be clear after the seizure.
(*Essentials of Lenin*, Vol. II, p. 140.)

The fundamental question of every revolution is the question of state power, said Lenin. If he could once get his hands
on the state apparatus he felt certain that power could be retained,—"even tomorrow events may put power into our
hands, and then we shall not relinquish it." (*Collected Works*,
Vol. XXI, Book I, p. 138.) If power could once be gained,
terror would make certain that it would not be lost.

Here there must be a terroristic purging; summary
trial and the firing squad . . . terror cannot be dispensed with notwithstanding the hypocrites and
phrasemongers. (*Essentials of Lenin*, Vol. II, p. 722.)

The place for Mensheviks and Socialist-Revolutionaries, open or disguised as non-party, is in prison. . . .
Let those who want to play at parliamentarism, at Constituent Assemblies, at non-party conferences, go
abroad. . . . We have no time to play at "oppositions"
at "conferences." (*Essentials of Lenin*, Vol. II, p.
727.)

It was not bravado but determination that led Lenin to
state that power, once gained, would never be surrendered.

We, the Bolshevik Party, have *convinced* Russia. We
have won Russia from the rich for the poor, from
the exploiters for the toilers. Now we must *administer*
Russia. (Lenin, *Selected Works*, Vol. VII, p. 316.)

Lenin has properly been called an "engineer of revolution,"
for without him the *coup d'état* of October would never have
taken place. But he was more. He was a lifelong student of
power, a genius with regard to its seizure *and its retention.*
He was the first man to envision the modern totalitarian state
in any detail. He drew up the blueprints, worked out the
theory. A careful examination of his writings shows that
there are few dictatorial techniques now known which are not
to be found there, developed to a greater or lesser degree.

The passages from *State and Revolution* quoted in Chapter
V are written in the anti-state, super-democratic tone, characteristic of most of that important work. Woven into many of
these passages, however, often unobtrusively, is a second
strand of thought.

Given these *economic* premises it is quite possible,
after the overthrow of the capitalists and bureaucrats,
to proceed immediately, overnight, to supersede them
in the *control* of production and distribution, in the
work of *keeping account* of labour and products by the
armed workers, by the whole of the armed population . . .

Accounting and control—that is the *main* thing required for the "setting up" and correct functioning of

the first phase of Communist society. *All* citizens are transformed into the salaried employees of the state, which consists of the armed workers. *All citizens* become employees and workers of a *single* national state "syndicate." All that is required is that they should work equally—do their proper share of work—and get paid equally. The accounting and control necessary for this have been *simplified* by capitalism to an extreme and reduced to the extraordinarily simple operations— which any literate person can perform—of checking and recording, knowledge of the four rules of arithmetic, and issuing receipts.

When the *majority* of the people begin independently and everywhere to keep such accounts and maintain such control over the capitalists (now converted into employees) and over the intellectual gentry who preserve their capitalist habits, this control will really become universal, general, national; and there will be no way of getting away from it, there will be "nowhere to go."

The whole of society will have become a single office and a single factory, with equality of labour and equality of pay.

But this "factory" discipline, which the proletariat will extend to the whole of society after the defeat of the capitalists and the overthrow of the exploiters, is by no means our ideal, or our ultimate goal. It is but a necessary *step* for the purpose of thoroughly purging society of all the hideousness and foulness of capitalist exploitation, *and for further progress*. (*Essentials of Lenin*, Vol. II, p. 210.)

Lenin speaks here of accounting being done "by the whole of the armed population." He speaks of the "*majority* of the people" beginning "independently and everywhere to keep such accounts," and maintain controls. These statements represent his bow in the direction of direct democracy and the class will theory. Marx had said that after the revolution the "masses themselves" would perform all the tasks of governing. In order to make this view appear plausible, Lenin had to make the further preposterous assumption that the tasks of government had been reduced to the "extraordinarily simple operations—which any literate person can perform—of checking and recording, knowledge of the four rules of arithmetic, and issuing receipts."

The second strand of thought, however, is grim rather than preposterous. Interspersed among the super-democratic passages are passages calling for the possession of startling powers by central authorities, powers that are, so far as can be seen, completely unchecked. Lenin speaks of "*control* of production and distribution," and states that "all citizens are transformed into the salaried employees of the state." "All citizens become employees and workers of a *single* national 'syndicate'." Control will be "universal, general, national." The "whole of society will have become a single office and a single factory." He refers in the final lines to " 'factory' discipline" which the proletariat will "extend to the whole of society."

It was to be expected that this second strand of thought should be present. The writings of Marx and Engels are pervaded by an animus toward the state but political rule requires an acceptance of the state. Before the members of the Bolshevik faction of the Russian Social Democratic Labor Party could be psychologically prepared to rule Russia their minds had to be freed from subservience to the anti-state views of the founders of Marxism. *State and Revolution* was Lenin's major effort to restore the state to respectability in Bolshevik eyes. In that work, however, he far more than redressed the balance.

Lenin could not attack the Marxian view of the state frontally and demonstrate its absurdity without opening himself to charges of heresy. Since he could not storm the citadel he had no alternative but to seek to take it by stratagem. All his demands for state control, consequently, even the most thoroughgoing, are put forward in the name of democracy or reform or of "really revolutionary" action.

What is universal labour service?

It is a step forward on the basis of modern monopoly capitalism, a step towards the regulation of economic life as a whole in accordance with a certain general plan, a step towards the economy of national labour and towards the prevention of its senseless wastage by capitalism.

In Germany it is the Junkers (landlords) and capitalists who are introducing universal labour service, and therefore it inevitably becomes military servitude for the workers.

But take the same institution and ponder over its significance in a revolutionary-democratic state. Universal labour service, introduced, regulated and directed by the Soviets of Workers', Soldiers', and Peasants' Deputies, will *not yet* be Socialism, but it will *no longer* be capitalism. It will be a tremendous *step towards Socialism* . . . (*Essentials of Lenin*, Vol. II, p. 114.)

In Germany, universal labor service was military service for the workers. In Russia the same phenomenon is a "step forward," a "tremendous step toward socialism."

During the extraordinary sufferings the country is going through, and in order to fight the impending catastrophe, a revolutionary-democratic policy would not confine itself to bread cards, but would add, first, compulsory organisation of the population into consumers' societies, for without such an organisation it is impossible fully to introduce control over consumption; secondly, it would introduce the labor duty for the rich with the proviso that they must provide these consumers' societies with secretarial and other labour free of charge; thirdly, it would introduce among the

population equal distribution of all articles of consumption without exception, so that the burdens of
the war may really be equally distributed; fourthly, it
would introduce such organisation of control that the
consumption of the rich would be controlled by the
poor classes of the population.

The introduction of real democracy in this realm,
the manifestation of the real revolutionary spirit in the
organisation of control on the part of the neediest
classes of the people, would serve as a great stimulus
towards straining every available intelligent force, towards developing the really revolutionary energy of the
whole people. (Lenin, *Collected Works*, Vol. XXI,
Book I, p. 202.)

Labor duty for "the rich" is to be introduced. But who is
to decide who is rich and who is not? The population is to
be organized into consumers' societies. By whom? Control is
to be extended over "all articles of consumption without exception," but who is to exert this life and death control over
the members of society? The consumption of the rich is to be
controlled by the poor. How are "the poor," perhaps sixty
million people, perhaps one hundred and sixty million, to
make the numerous, detailed decisions necessary to execute
such a scheme? In every case the answer comes down to the
state, controlled, of course, by the Party. Although Lenin
writes in the democratic-sounding class will vein, and terms
this the introduction of "real democracy," the picture emerging is unmistakably that of the modern totalitarian state.

The state is an organ or apparatus of force to be used
by one class against another. So long as it remains an
apparatus for the bourgeoisie to use force against the
proletariat, so long can the slogan of the proletariat
be only—the *destruction* of this state. But when the
state has become proletarian, when it has become an
apparatus of force to be used by the proletariat against
the bourgeoisie, then we shall be fully and unreservedly

for a strong state power and centralism. (Lenin, *Collected Works*, Vol. XXI, Book II, p. 39.)

As long as Communists do not control the state apparatus they must agitate for its destruction. When they have succeeded in seizing power, however, they will be in favor of firm authority and central control.

To prove to the Bolsheviks, who are centralists by conviction and by the programme and tactics of their whole party, the need of centralism means really to break into an open door. (Lenin, *Collected Works*, Vol. XXI, Book II, p. 38.)

If it seems an overstatement to say that the outlines of the modern totalitarian state can be seen emerging from Lenin's pre-October writings, other passages can be quoted.

The grain monopoly, the bread cards, universal labour service become, in the hands of the proletarian state, in the hands of the all-powerful Soviets, the most powerful means for accounting and control, a means which, extended to the capitalists and *the rich in general*, being applied to them by the *workers*, will give a power unheard-of in history for "setting in motion" the state apparatus, for overcoming the resistance of the capitalists, for subjecting them to the proletarian state. This means of control and compulsory *labour* is stronger than the laws of the Convention and its guillotine. The guillotine only frightened, only crushed *active* resistance. *For us this is not enough.*
. . . We must not only "frighten" the capitalists so that they feel the all-pervading strength of the proletarian state and forget to think of active resistance to it. We must crush also their *passive* resistance, which is undoubtedly still more dangerous and harmful . . .

And we have the means to do so. The belligerent capitalist state has itself given us the means to carry this out. This means is the grain monopoly, the bread cards, universal labour service. "He who works not, neither shall he eat." (Lenin, *Collected Works*, Vol. XXI, Book II, p. 32.)

The state is to possess a monopoly of the grain and to ration it as it sees fit. This will, says Lenin, as a man who has studied these things, "give a power unheard-of in history." It will represent the application of modern techniques of control to the ancient task of dictatorship.

If it be argued that it is a mistake to see in a passage like this the shadow of Stalin's labor camps and the institutionalization of hunger as a means of control, it is only necessary to quote from Lenin's "Proletarian Revolution and the Renegade Kautsky," written *after* the seizure of power.

> And if you, exploiters, attempt to offer resistance to our proletarian revolution we will ruthlessly suppress you; we will deprive you of all rights; more than that, we will not give you any bread ... for we are Socialists in real earnest . . . (*Essentials of Lenin*, Vol. II, p. 399.)

The controls that Lenin demanded before the seizure were never fully effective during his lifetime, but that was not through lack of effort on his part.

> 5. Universal labour service is hereby introduced: all citizens of both sexes between the ages of sixteen and fifty-five shall be obliged to perform work assigned to them by the local Soviets of Workers', Soldiers' and Peasants' Deputies, or by other organs of the Soviet power.
>
> 7. For the purpose of proper control and distribution of foodstuffs and other necessary products, every citizen of the state shall be obliged to join a consumers' society. ("Draft Decree on Socialisation of the National Economy, December 1917," reprinted in *Essentials of Lenin*, Vol. II, pp. 251-52.)

A certain amount of time will inevitably pass before the masses . . . will understand and *feel* that without an all-sided state accounting and control of production and distribution of goods, the power of the toilers and the freedom of the toilers, cannot be maintained, and that a return to the yoke of capitalism is inevitable. (*Selected Works*, Vol. VII, pp. 327-28.)

And when a Menshevik says: "You are now retreating; I have been in favor of retreat all the time, I agree with you, I am your man, let us retreat together," we say in reply: "For the public advocacy of Menshevism our revolutionary courts must pass sentence of death, otherwise they are not our courts, but God knows what." . . . had we listened to what they said we should have been unable to hold power for two months. Indeed, the sermons which . . . the Mensheviks and Socialist-Revolutionaries preach express their true natures: "The revolution has gone too far. What you are saying now we have been saying all the time, permit us to say it again." But we say in reply: "Permit us to put you against the wall for saying that. Be good enough to refrain from expressing your views." (Lenin, *Essentials*, Vol. II, pp. 784-785.)

The control that Lenin sought over men's bodies he sought over their minds as well. He once said, in absolute contradiction to a basic Marxian tenet, "Without a revolutionary theory there can be no revolutionary movement... (*Essentials*, Vol. II, pp. 47-48.) This statement sums up his attitude toward Marxist theory and his understanding of the role that that body of doctrine could play as a "myth," in the sense that Sorel used the term. Lenin has not been alone in his understanding of the nature and function of myths. Mussolini and Hitler also perceived that men could be moved to action by doctrines quite divorced from reality. Mussolini wrote of this insight many times.

We have created our myth. The myth is a faith, it is a passion. It is not necessary that it shall be a reality. . . . Our myth is the Nation, our myth is the greatness of the nation! (Quoted in Finer, Herman, *Mussolini's Italy*, New York: Henry Holt & Co., 1935, p. 218.)

Mussolini speaks as an acute psychologist but as an obtuse politician. He understood that men will believe doctrines having little resemblance to reality but he did not understand that they will cease to believe when they discover how slight the resemblance is. Men will believe things which are untrue but they will not believe those things which they know to be untrue. By pointing out that the doctrine of the Nation was a myth created by himself to serve as a lever in moving men, Mussolini seriously undermined the effectiveness of that very myth. Lenin, on the other hand, instead of parading the fact that the Marxian scheme was a myth, a series of fictions, always insisted that it was wholly and completely true.

The teaching of Marx is all-powerful because it is true. It is complete and symmetrical, offering an integrated view of the world, irreconcilable with any superstition, with any reactionism, or with any defense of bourgeois oppression. (Lenin, "The Three Sources and the Three Constituent Parts of Marxism," reprinted in *Capital and Other Writings of Karl Marx*, p. xxi.)

You cannot eliminate even one basic assumption, one substantial part of this philosophy of Marxism (it is as if it were a solid block of steel) without abandoning objective truth, without falling into the arms of the bourgeois-reactionary falsehood. (Lenin, *Materialism and Empiro-Criticism*, New York: International Publishers, 1927, p. 281.)

There are numerous elements in the Marxist and Marxist-Leninist schemes that have as little resemblance to reality as the avowed myths of racial purity, primeval blood, and the "Aryan race." Such fictions as the following have been touched on: the dogma that all processes in nature develop dialectically; the idea that there exist monolithic and hostile "classes" of the sort described by Marx; the idea that "class" conflict is the basis of all history; the idea that a "classless society" must inevitably develop out of the struggle of two of these classes; the idea that a mystical bond of "class consciousness" makes the Communist Party somehow devoted to the interests of the working people; the idea that the "proletariat" has triumphed in Russia; the idea that the *coup d'état* of October 1917 was the "proletarian revolution" foretold by Marx; the idea that the workers and peasants rule the Soviet Union; the idea that there is genuine freedom and democracy in the Soviet Union; the idea that all nations not ruled by the Communist Party are ruled by banks and "financial consortiums" and so on. Never have Lenin and Stalin acknowledged these fictions for what they are, however. They have understood that a myth system cannot be adhered to with religious passion unless it is believed to be objectively true and they have, consequently, insisted on the identity of their theoretical formulations with reality.

Many persons have pointed out that Marxism is, among other things, a secular religion. It has in History its God, in Marx its Prophet, in Engels, Lenin and Stalin its Saints; its Priesthood in the Party, the World Revolution as its Day of Judgment, the Proletariat as its Chosen People, "primitive communism" as its Garden of Eden, the classless society as its Promised Land, and so on. It fills many of the same functions psychologically speaking, that a religion does. For those who can believe, it provides certain knowledge. Its faithful can, on all questions, enjoy the "deep slumber of decided opinion." No doubt or uncertainty need ever penetrate. The whole significance of history is known, its beginnings, its present tendencies and its certain end. Nothing is unknown about man's relation to his fellow men or to the universe.

While it has been perceived that many people adhere to Marxism with a religious intensity, the significance of the fact that the Marxist religion is the official religion of the Communist Party has not been perceived. The Party's war against the traditional religions in the areas under its control has been presented, and accepted, as merely one more episode in the age-old contest between church and state.

The Party cannot be neutral towards religion, and it does conduct anti-religious propaganda against all and every religious prejudice because it stands for science while religious prejudices run counter to science, because all religion is something opposite to science. . . . The Party cannot be neutral towards the bearers of religious prejudices, towards the reactionary clergy who poison the minds of the toiling masses. Have we suppressed the reactionary clergy? Yes, we have. The unfortunate thing is that it has not been completely liquidated. (*Leninism*, Vol. II, p. 70.)

Does that mean the Party is neutral towards religion? No, it does not. We carry on and will continue to carry on propaganda against religious prejudices. Our legislation guarantees to citizens the right to adhere to any religion. This is a matter for the conscience of each individual. That is precisely why we carried out the separation of Church from the State. But in separating the Church from the State and proclaiming religious liberty, we at the same time guarantee the right of every citizen to combat by argument, by propaganda, and agitation any and all religion. (*Ibid.*)

The "freedom of anti-religious propaganda" that is guaranteed, however, is freedom to oppose any religion *but* the Marxist-Leninist religion. *That* religion is called a science and the Party defends it against all attack. The leaders of the Party will not tolerate the propagation of any views that threaten the series of fictions by means of which they justify their dictatorial rule. The Party's war on traditional religions is significant, not as an example of the state-church conflict, but because it represents the use of state power by the adherents of one religion as a means of exterminating the adherents of all other religions.

Marxism was a religion from its inception but Lenin made it the *official* religion of his combination political party, religious order and private army. The result was that when the Bolsheviks seized the state apparatus in 1917, religious and secular powers were joined, *church and state became one.* The fiction of the separation of church and state in the Soviet Union has been maintained so effectively that the actual amalgamation of the two has scarcely been perceived. The Party can be described as a political-military organization that has taken over the functions of a church, or as a church militant that has effected a seizure of secular power. Communist rule can be described equally well as representing the absorption of the church by the state or the obliteration of the state by the church. The important realization is that the religious and political spheres have been joined, that Marxism-Leninism is a civil religion having as its principal function the support and justification of Communist rule.

When these two spheres are fused, as they have been in the Soviet Union, there ceases to be any possibility of competition between church and state for the loyalty of the individual. The demands of the two cannot conflict, since the religion— tailor-made to suit the purposes of the Dictator—teaches that the highest duty of the individual is to submit to secular power.

When people talk to us about morality, we say: for the Communist, morality lies entirely in this compact, united discipline and conscious mass struggle against the exploiters. We do not believe in an eternal morality, and we expose all the fables about morality. (*Essentials of Lenin*, Vol. II, p. 670.)

Morality for us is subordinated to the interests of the class struggle of the proletariat. (*Ibid.*, p. 668.)

We say that our morality is entirely subordinated to the interests of the class struggle of the proletariat. (*Ibid.*, p. 667.)

Instead of the schools being separate from the church, as alleged, they are completely under its control:

> The basis of Communist morality is the struggle for the consolidation and completion of Communism. That is also the basis of Communist training, education, and teaching. That is the reply to the question of how Communism should be learnt. (*Ibid.,* p. 670.)

When secular and religious authority center in one institution, in this case the Party, enormous power is concentrated in the hands that control that institution. The claims of the church can never act as a check on the claims of the state since the two are one. The religious leader will never prescribe duties different from those prescribed by the secular leader since the two leaders are one.

The Dictator, as head of the Church-State, has control over both the minds and bodies of his subjects. He controls the *press*, the *radio* and the *education system*. He controls *travel*. He controls the *secret police* and he controls the *military power* of the country. His organization has a monopoly of *political activity* and a monopoly of decision with regard to all significant *economic* matters. The state rules society, the party rules the state, and the Dictator rules the Party. The reins of all power are gathered in his hands. There is no power like it on earth. It is the Leviathan, the Juggernaut, the modern Totalitarian State.

CHAPTER XII

The Great Illusion

COMMUNISM has been called "the great illusion of our time." The description is at bottom accurate although Communism is actually a whole fabric of illusions rather than a single one. The responsibility for the fabrication of the majority of these illusions belongs to Lenin, and the ease with which they won wide acceptance is explained, in part, by an illusion having to do with Lenin himself—the idea that he was devoted to freedom and welfare for the working people of the world.

So long as Lenin is regarded as having been a fighter for the "common man" his true character and abilities will never be understood and Stalin will be credited with originating dictatorial techniques that are really Lenin's. As long as Lenin is accepted as a humanitarian revolutionary, resort will have to be made to the involved theory of "betrayal" to explain the evolution of the "workers' democracy" into a totalitarian society. According to this theory, all was well in Russia while Lenin lived. His "excesses" are explained away as simply a manifestation of his burning desire to create a new, more perfect, world. After Lenin's death, as this theory would have it, the ruthless Asiatic villain, Stalin, seized power and proceeded to undo all of Lenin's good work, betraying Lenin and betraying "socialism."

This theory has the merit of justifying the conduct of those persons who supported the Communist movement while it was young but who have now renounced it. Instead of forcing the disenchanted to acknowledge an earlier naïveté, it allows them to maintain that it is Communism that has changed, not they. The flaw in this argument is the fact that not *discon-*

tinuity, but a high degree of *continuity*, joins the regimes of the two men. It is not distortion that allows Stalin to justify much of what he has done by citing the speeches and writings of Lenin, and it is no accident that the two-volume edition of Stalin's most important work should be entitled "Leninism." Lenin was the teacher and Stalin is no more than an apt pupil.

If Lenin had been unsuccessful in his bid for power he might have written a new *Prince* in which the outlines of the modern totalitarian state would have been clearly set forth for the first time. As it was, he engaged in political activity until his death and could not, therefore, afford to systematize his methods and perceptions. Consequently, his importance as a prophet of totalitarianism has not been perceived, and he is treated more often as a democrat who failed than as a dictator who was brilliantly successful.

That Lenin should continue to be regarded by many persons as a man who was concerned with freedom and plenty for the working masses is a significant commentary on his insight as a theoretician of dictatorship and on his skill as a practitioner of it. Understanding the appeal that democratic ideas had for his audience, he rarely failed to deck out his demands in the language of democracy. Few men have proclaimed their love for freedom more fiercely and frequently than the totalitarian Lenin. He appeared to act on the principle of never opposing a sentiment that could be put to use. He did not say that he was against democratic ideas but, rather, that he was for them. The Communists would, for the first time, he said, give these concepts a "real" content. When he finished redefining them there was, of course, little left. They were gutted in the process of being made "real."

In Russia in 1917 there were elements paving the way for the evolution of the arbitrary state power that exists today and there were present, at the same time, the foundations on which a democratic society might have been erected. Neither set of factors was so predominant as to make impossible the

tipping of the scales in the other direction. The future of
Russia and, consequently, the future of the world, hung in
the balance that year and the factor that proved decisive was
not a great historical force but a single man—Lenin.

If Lenin has been such a pivotal figure in the creation of
Communism, what role is left for Marx, its nominal founder?
If Marx's shade were to return today it would almost certainly
not approve of modern communism. Nevertheless, because
the scheme which Marx devised was capable of such ready
conversion to Lenin's purposes, a degree of responsibility
must necessarily rest on his shoulders. By his lack of political
realism and his failure to deal with important problems, Marx
set the stage for the subversion of his own creation. If Marx's
shade should ever reproach Lenin's, the latter would be able
to reply in the words of Dostoievsky's Grand Inquisitor:
"Thou didst Thyself lay the foundations for the destruction
of Thy kingdom, and no man is more to blame for it. . . ."
No man but Lenin, that is.

Though Marx created the scheme in the first instance, it
was Lenin who perceived how easily it could be converted to
dictatorial purposes despite its democratic appearance. The
Marxian system contains democratic and anti-democratic elements and both have been used to provide the theoretical
justification for political movements. While the leaders of the
various socialist parties made use of the democratic elements
and ignored the other, Lenin seized on the anti-democratic
elements and used the democratic elements solely as a smoke-
screen. In Lenin's hands Marxian doctrine became a superb
instrument for confusing and dividing those who attempted
to resist his power or the power of the Bolsheviks. His treatment of the question of "socialism" and his use of the notion
of "class" are two cases in point.

The word "socialism" has commonly been used to refer to
"social" ownership of the means of production and distribution, it being taken for granted that this control was to be
democratically exercised. Since the proviso of democratic con-

trol is usually tacitly rather than explicitly expressed, it is easily overlooked. Once it is overlooked, once "socialism" is thought of *simply* as state control of a nation's economic life, it becomes quite compatible with totalitarianism, it becomes, in fact, merely one aspect of the total control of society by the state. By ignoring the proviso of democratic control, or, rather, by assuming that Party control is in the nature of things democratic, Lenin and Stalin have been able to present their totalitarian rule as the "socialism" desired by so many liberal and humane persons.

It is not socialism or real democracy that Lenin and Stalin have achieved but total control over Russian society. By their talk of socialism and democracy, however, they have succeeded in screening their motives and in dividing those who should have been united against them. Because they have called their totalitarianism "socialism," they have been able to take advantage of the sentiment in favor of socialism and, at the same time, denounce those who oppose their tyranny as opponents of socialism. A simple device, yet one that has proved extremely effective.

Marx saw the world as convulsed by a conflict between two giant antagonists, the proletariat and the bourgeoisie. He envisioned this conflict as taking place in every industrialized society without regard to geographic boundaries. By proclaiming "class" divisions as the only significant divisions in modern society and class wars as the only significant conflicts, Marx gave to his doctrine what might be called a horizontal appeal as opposed to a vertical or national appeal.* This horizontal orientation prevented the Marxian scheme from becoming linked to a single nation during the lifetimes of Marx and Engels.

Lenin and Stalin, in keeping with their technique of portraying the real world as if it were the world which Marx

*Marx's astounding lack of concern for nation states, then as now phenomena of tremendous importance, is to be explained, like many other curious aspects of his system, by the paralyzing effect that his formal scheme had on his powers of observation—a matter treated in Chapter V.

created, have maintained the fiction of a globe divided into a "socialist" camp on the one hand and a "capitalist" camp on the other. The important difference is, however, that Lenin and Stalin have sought to link the alleged struggle between the two camps to a geographic base. After the Bolshevik seizure of power in 1917 Lenin enunciated the doctrine of the "socialist fatherland," and thus combined vertical and horizontal, national and super-national appeals. The idea was that since the "proletariat" had seized power in Russia that country was properly the spiritual home of "proletarians" everywhere. Marxian doctrine was thus anchored to a single country, to the great benefit of the masters of that country. Lenin and Stalin have been able to use nationalist appeals at home while using the horizontal class doctrine to persuade citizens of other nations that they owe their primary allegiance, not to their own "bourgeois" societies, but to the Soviet Union, the land of the proletariat.*

The cooperation that Moscow expects from a Communist in a non-Communist country extends to support of the Soviet Union against his own country in the event of war. The line of reasoning is that since the proletariat rules in the Soviet Union and since all wars are class wars, any war in which the Soviet Union participates must be a war of the proletariat against the bourgeoisie.

---

*One of the basic weaknesses of this doctrine as an instrument of Soviet imperialism is its instability. Since Marx and Engels did not attach the system which they fashioned to a single country, it is always possible for courageous Communists outside the Soviet Union who are weary of Moscow's insistence on absolute obedience, to appeal from the Leninist-Stalinist version of Marxism to the original doctrine. Thus Marshal Tito could, with justification, ask why the ukase of the Communist Party of the Soviet Union should be accepted as binding by the Communist parties of other countries. That he survived the asking of the question is, of course, explained solely by the fact that he was well entrenched in Yugoslavia. The argument between the Cominform and Tito was carried on at the level of theory but, as always in these battles, power was the decisive point. The division of opinion followed the boundary line between Yugoslav and Soviet power. Tito's arguments were accepted as compelling by the Yugoslavs while Moscow's reasoning was accepted by all non-Yugoslav Iron Curtain Communists as unassailable.

. Socialism is opposed to violence against nations. That is indisputable. But Socialism is opposed to violence against men in general. Apart from Christian-anarchists and Tolstoyans, however, no one has yet drawn the conclusion from this that Socialism is opposed to *revolutionary* violence. Hence, to talk about "violence" in general, without examining the conditions which distinguish reactionary from revolutionary violence, means being a petty bourgeois who renounces revolution, or else it means simply deceiving oneself and others by sophistry.

The same holds true of violence against nations. Every war implies violence against nations, but that does not prevent Socialists from being in *favour* of a revolutionary war. The class character of war—that is the fundamental question which confronts a Socialist (if he is not a renegade). (*Essentials of Lenin*, Vol. II, p. 402-403.)

The Soviet Union is, by definition, never the aggressor. Even when its armies invade non-communist countries those countries are termed "aggressors," and it becomes the duty of Communists in them to aid the fight of the progressive class against reaction, that is, to assist the invasion by all means at their disposal.*

*The following are statements by spokesmen of the French, Italian and United States Communist Parties:
" . . . if the Soviet Army, defending the cause of freedom and of socialism, should be brought to pursue the aggressors onto our soil, could the workers and people of France have any other attitude toward the Soviet Army than has been that of the peoples of Poland, Rumania and Yugoslavia?" (Maurice Thorez, *N. Y. Times*, Feb. 23, 1949.)
"I think that in this case the Italian people who cannot but condemn all aggressions would have the evident duty of helping the Soviet Army in the most effective way possible to give the aggressor the lesson he deserves. . . . As one can see this would not be a national war but a typical war of social classes and ideologies, a war of reaction and capitalists against social progress and the workers. It is evident in this case what the position should be of those who are for social progress and socialism against reaction." (Palmiro Togliatti, *N. Y. Times*, Feb. 27, 1949.)

Jargon such as this is, however, coming to be seen for what it is,—a highly formalistic mode of speaking designed to convey one meaning to the initiated and quite another to the uninitiated. To understand its real meaning a novice must first go slowly, substituting a whole series of special definitions for common words, much as if he were mastering a new language, as indeed he is. In time his facility with the language will increase and he will be able to translate the jargon, to decipher it, as rapidly as a trained Communist can encode it. When he is completely at home in the language he will find that its principal function is to enable Communists to stand the world on its head, to make black appear white.

The world has been divided into two hostile camps, truly enough, but not by the issue of socialism versus capitalism. Were this the important issue, as the Communists insist, socialist nations would certainly not be found in the "capitalist" camp. That such a relatively minor question has been so widely accepted as the main point at issue and that so many books and articles have explored in complete seriousness the question of whether "capitalist" and "socialist" economies (meaning Russia's economy) could coexist is eloquent testimony of the extent to which non-Marxists have been led to accept the fallacious Communist statement of the problem.

The important issue today is between freedom and democracy, however imperfectly achieved, on the one hand, and tyranny and terror on the other. The masters of the Soviet Union are not seeking to create a socialist society or a classless society or to extend the power of the underprivileged. They are seeking, rather, the indefinite extension of their own power by every available means.

The charges that Communist leaders level at others are, as often as not, precisely the charges to which Communism itself

"We're not going to fight against the Soviet Union. . . . We are not going to fight in any imperialistic war. . . . I do not consider the Soviet Union an enemy. The only possibility of the Soviets going to war with the United States would be if the United States declared war." (William Z. Foster, *N. Y. Times*, May 29, 1949.)

is vulnerable. It is a Communist charge, for example, that "bourgeois" governments are incapable of dealing with significant social problems. Had Marx been less preoccupied with formula and dogma he might have perceived how precarious is economic privilege in a society based on political democracy. For Stalin to echo these charges today is to ignore the history of the past century with its numerous examples of the way in which political democracies have, in fact, shown themselves able to deal with serious social and economic problems. As long as democratic procedures are maintained there is a means at hand for forcing the attention of governments to the needs of their people. In the Soviet Union political democracy does not exist and no such means is available. It is the Soviet Union, then, rather than countries like the United States and Great Britain that possesses a rigid governmental structure.

The governments of democratic countries can change peacefully but it is unthinkable that the masters of the Soviet Union should give up their power voluntarily. The structure is so rigid that even if they desired to do so, they could not make significant concessions without bringing the entire edifice down around their ears. The price of concession is prohibitive. Communist rule is maintained by unceasing propaganda backed by the generous application of force. If that force were even momentarily relaxed the Party and its leaders would be swept away in a flood. If the great weight of totalitarian repression were once loosened, that apparently monolithic organization would dissolve overnight into the natural diversity of men in society. Soviet unity is spurious rather than genuine, the appearance rather than the reality. It represents an inability to accept diversity and is, consequently, less stable than a seemingly less unified democratic society based on an acceptance of diversity.

Stalin maintains that "bourgeois" governments are indifferent to the interests of the people while Communist governments strive always to improve the lot of the people. How different is the reality! Communists justify their crimes in the name of a better society, but those crimes are *irrelevant* to the achievement of a better society, and always have been. It is a shattering realization, but the whole thing has been a hoax. The millions of persons killed in the name of a better world have contributed not to the achievement of that goal but only to the maintenance of the Communist dictatorship.

Stalin maintains that the "bourgeois" nations possess only "formal" democracy. Yet where is it that democratic procedures are truly sheer formality? He maintains that the freedoms enjoyed by the people of those nations are sham freedoms. Yet where is it that the government controls the press, the radio, travel and assembly? Where is it that men are taken at night never to be heard from again while their families are in too great terror even to inquire what has become of them?

This is not a blanket denial of Communist charges against the United States, the stronghold of resistance to Communism. Ideal democracy has not been achieved in this country or in any other country. There is a great deal to be done at present, and strive as we may, there will always remain a great deal to be done. Many of the charges made by Communists possess, therefore, elements of truth. This must not be denied merely because we dislike having the matter brought to our attention by Communists or because an admission of imperfection might, at first glance, appear to weaken our position in the struggle against Communism.

It is true that many persons have in the past contrasted, to our detriment, our confessions of imperfection with the Soviet Union's claims to perfection. But if we have been put at a disadvantage by the admission that our reality falls short of our ideals, the spokesmen of the Soviet Union have been put in a far more difficult position by their insistence that the Soviet reality does *not* fall short of its ideals. Because we admit imperfection we are not forced to falsify reality. Because the Communists do not admit imperfection they *must* falsify reality. With the discrepancy between the ideal and the actuality as glaring as it is now, it is becoming increasingly difficult to present the one as the other with any hope of success.

This study, an attempt to explore the inner workings of Communism, has now come to an end. It is the author's hope that the reader's understanding of Communism has been advanced, that he has penetrated the disguise of Communism and has seen it for what it is—evil masquerading as good.

Appendix

I. IDEOLOGY

According to Marx's theory of ideology, men think and act as their class position dictates. A worker is supposed to adhere to proletarian, i.e. Communist, beliefs and an employer of wage-labor is supposed to adhere to a bourgeois ideology. Since, as was pointed out in Chapter I, there exists no mechanism capable of producing this correspondence, many persons do not, in fact, believe as their class position would indicate that they should.

Marx's problem, consequently, was that of accounting for the discrepancy between his theory and reality without surrendering his determinist psychology and with it a great deal of his theoretical structure. It was impossible that the problem should be dealt with satisfactorily. If the determinist psychology were true, a discrepancy between class position on the one hand and beliefs on the other would automatically be ruled out. Conversely, if discrepancies between class position and beliefs did exist, then the determinist psychology could not be true. Marx had two courses open to him. He could ignore the discrepancy between beliefs and class position and assume that his theory was an adequate description of reality, or, he could acknowledge the discrepancy and try to explain it in some way that would not undermine any important theoretical assumptions. He did both.

For the most part, the intensity of Marx's belief appears to have blinded him to the very existence of discrepancies. He commonly ignored them and wrote instead as if all workers and manufacturers thought and acted as, according to his scheme, they should. Occasionally, however, Marx tacitly recognized the facts and tried to explain how it happened that many workers have "bourgeois" beliefs and many bourgeois have "proletarian" beliefs.

One of the ways in which he sought to deal with the first part of this problem was to suggest that those workers who were not Communists were somehow not "real" workers at all. This distinction in no way solves the difficulty. To make it is to acknowledge that the determinist psychology is faulty. If the reflection mechanism existed there would be no need for a distinction between "real" workers, i.e. Communists, and ordinary workers, since all workers would be Communists.

A second way in which Marx sought to explain the discrepancy was by contending that all workers who are not Communists must be bribed tools of the capitalists. This class-traitor explanation is equally inconsistent with Marx's basic psychological assumptions. If a man's loyalties are determined by his class position in the iron fashion which Marx customarily takes for granted, then it is surely out of the question that a simple desire for financial gain should in any way alter them. According to the reflection theory, a man not only could not switch from one ideology to another if he desired, he could not even want to make such a shift.

When it comes to explaining why some members of the bourgeoisie have cast their lot in with the proletariat, Marx finds an explanation more flattering than that of being a traitor to one's class. This is not to be wondered at since both Marx and Engels were, by their own account, bourgeois.

Finally, in times when the class-struggle nears the decisive hour, the process of dissolution going on within the ruling class—in fact, within the whole range of an old society—assumes such a violent, glaring character that a small section of the ruling class cuts itself adrift and joins the revolutionary class, the class that holds the future in its hands. Just as, therefore, at an earlier period, a section of the nobility went over to the bourgeoisie, so now a portion of the bourgeoisie goes over to the proletariat, and in particular, a portion of the bourgeois ideologists, who have raised themselves to the level of comprehending theoretically the historical movements as a whole. (*Communist Manifesto*, p. 331.)

This doctrine is quite as incompatible with the Marxian determinist psychology as the two preceding explanations. If thoughts and actions are determined by class position, how can a section of one class "cut itself adrift" and join the enemy? How could a mental perception, such as that of the dissolution going on within a class, counter the overwhelming force of class position? And, if beliefs are simply reflections of class position, how is it even possible for an "ideologist" of one class to raise himself to the level of "comprehending theoretically" the movement of history as a whole? If an individual can cut himself adrift from his class as easily as the class-traitor and historical insight doctrines suggest, then there can exist no rigidity between class lines and people are free to shift from one class to another as the spirit moves them.

When Marx ignores the discrepancies he is true to his determinist psychology but at the price of losing touch with reality. When he seeks to explain the discrepancies, he accommodates reality but at the cost of tacitly recognizing the falsity of his psychological theory.

II. FREEDOM AND NECESSITY

It has often been pointed out that though Marx and Engels speak of iron historical laws they frequently make appeals for revolutionary action.

The Communists disdain to conceal their views and aims. They openly declare that their ends can be attained only by the forcible overthrow of all existing social conditions. Let the ruling classes tremble at a Communistic revolution. The proletarians have nothing to lose but their chains. They have a world to win.

Workingmen of all countries, unite! (*Communist Manifesto*, p. 355.)

The philosophers have only *interpreted* the world in various ways; the point however is to *change* it. (Marx, *Eleventh Thesis on Feuerbach*, reprinted in *Selected Works*, Vol. I, p. 354.)

. . . for the practical materialist, i.e., the communist, it is a question of revolutionizing the existing world, of practically attacking and changing existing things. (*German Ideology*, p. 34.)

In one breath Marx may maintain that the actions of all persons are determined by the means of production and in the next he may laud the "historical initiative" shown by those persons.

And this is what our heroic Party comrades in Paris are attempting. What elasticity, what historical initiative, what a capacity for sacrifice in these Parisians! . . . History has no like example of a like greatness. (Marx to Kugleman, *Selected Correspondence*, p. 309.)

The inconsistency between these two elements is so patent that many persons have felt that Marx and Engels must have had some way of harmonizing the two views. They were never harmonized, however, and they could not be, since they represent positions that are logically incompatible. If the one doctrine is true, the other cannot be.

A determinist scheme is, by its very nature, conservative. Hegel, the conservative, understood this aspect of the dialectic far better than did Marx and Engels. All three suffered from the conceit of believing that they had discovered the law of evolution of the universe and history, but Hegel at least had the insight to perceive that the dialectic was a support for conservative rather than revolutionary views. Marx and Engels assumed that the dialectic, as used by Hegel, was conservative only because history was presented as having already achieved its final goal.

Thus the revolutionary side (of the dialectic) becomes smothered beneath the overgrowth of the conservative side. . . . And so we find at the conclusion of the *Philosophy of Law* that the absolute idea is to be realized in that monarchy based on estates which Frederick III so persistently but so vainly promised his subjects. . . . (Engels, *Ludwig Feuerbach*, pp. 360-361.)

They thought they could de-conservatize the dialectic by shifting the emphasis from the present to the future, by stressing not the necessity of that which exists, but the necessity of the passing away of that which exists. No matter what specific content be inserted into the dialectical scheme, however, and no matter whether the emphasis be laid on the present or the future, the doctrine must always teach passivity and acquiescence since it teaches that history unfolds according to iron laws. It is this aspect of the dialectic that forces Marx and Engels to justify the existence of the bourgeoisie.

We see, therefore, how the modern bourgeoisie is itself the product of a long course of development, of a series of revolutions in the modes of production and of exchange. (*Communist Manifesto*, p. 323.)

The bourgeoisie, historically, has played a most revolutionary part. (*Ibid.*)

It [the bourgeoisie] has been the first to show what man's activity can bring about. It has accomplished wonders far surpassing Egyptian pyramids, Roman aqueducts and Gothic cathedrals . . . (*Ibid.*, p. 324.)

Not only must they justify its past existence, they must justify its present existence as well.

No social order ever disappears before all the productive forces, for which there is room in it, have been developed; and new, higher relations of production never appear before the material conditions of their existence have matured in the womb of the old society itself. (Preface to *A Contribution to the Critique of Political Economy*, p. 301.)

A phenomena which exists is, by the very fact of its existence, proved to be "necessary." Marx, the revolutionist, is forced to acknowledge the legitimacy of the very society which he hates. The most he can say is that while bourgeois society exists today, it will be obsolete tomorrow. Even though Marx and Engels built a revolution into History's unfolding their scheme remains fundamentally conservative.

Why then has it been so intimately associated with revolution in most minds? The explanation lies in the fact that the determinist element in the Marxian scheme has largely been ignored in practice. The appeals for action represent a concession to reality, a tacit acknowledgment that Marxist theory is one thing and reality another and that here can be no revolution until men act purposefully to bring it about. Marxism denies in practice the justification to the existing society which in theory it must grant. Everywhere in his writings Marx's ethical condemnation of bourgeois society is evident. In effect he states that bourgeois society is bad in spite of the fact that it exists. Marx the theoretician may point out that it is meaningless to criticize that which exists in terms of absolute values but the lesson is lost on Marx the revolutionary, whose writings are permeated with precisely that type of criticism.

III. CAUSATION IN THE MARXIAN SYSTEM

Only a few passages from the writings of Marx and Engels need be read for it to become apparent that causation in the Marxian system is quite different from causation as it is usually thought of.

> In these crises, the contradiction between social production and capitalist appropriation comes to a violent explosion. . . . The economic collision has reached its culminating point: *the mode of production rebels against the mode of exchange; the productive forces rebel against the mode of production, which they have outgrown.* (Engels, *Anti-Duhring*, p. 310.)
> The expanding force of the means of production bursts asunder the bonds imposed upon them by the

capitalist mode of production. Their release from these bonds . . . (*Ibid.*, p. 317.)

For many a decade past, the history of industry and commerce is but the history of the revolt of modern productive forces against modern conditions of production . . . (*Communist Manifesto*, p. 327.)

The new forces of production have already outgrown the bourgeois form of using them; and this conflict between productive forces and mode of production . . . (*Anti-Duhring*, p. 301.)

The monopoly of capital becomes a fetter upon the mode of production, which has sprung up and flourished along with, and under it. Centralisation of the means of production and socialisation of labour at last reach a point where they become incompatible with their capitalist integument. (*Capital*, Vol. I, p. 837.)

At a certain stage of their development, the material productive forces in society come in conflict with the existing relations of production. . . . From forms of development of the productive forces these relations turn into their fetters. (Preface to *A Contribution to the Critique of Political Economy*, reprinted in *Selected Works*, Vol. I, pp. 300-301.)

At a certain stage in the development of these means of production and of exchange . . . the feudal relations of property became no longer compatible with the already developed productive forces; they became so many fetters. (*Communist Manifesto*, p. 326.)

Instead of causal explanations in the usual sense, countless statements like those above are to be found. We see, for example, that the "contradiction" between social production and capitalist appropriation ends in a "violent explosion." The "economic collision" reaches its culminating point and the "mode of production" "rebels" against the "mode of exchange" and the "productive forces" "rebel" against the "mode of production" which they have "outgrown." The "expanding force" of the "means of production" "bursts asunder" the "bonds" imposed upon them by the capitalist mode of production. Another time the productive forces are presented as "revolting" against the conditions of production. The monopoly of capital is said to have become a "fetter" upon the mode of production and so on.

The striking thing about the above quoted passages, all of which deal with historical transitions that play an important part in the Marxian scheme, is their highly metaphorical nature. If their metaphorical nature is not immediately clear it becomes so as soon as an attempt is made to discover their precise meanings. What is the nature of the "contradiction" which is said to exist between socialist production and capitalist appropriation? How exactly does a mode of production "rebel" against a mode of exchange? Exactly how is it that a bodiless "relation" puts "fetters" on an intangible thing like a "force"? And what precisely is it that took place when feudal relations of property "burst asunder"?

A second striking feature of the writings of Marx and Engels is the frequency with which they attribute life and form to the entities with which they deal. In the passages quoted above the forces of production were spoken of as capable of being fettered, as capable, that is, of being put in leg and arm irons. "Free competition" is held to have "stepped" into the place of the relation of property. It was "accompanied" by two other entities which must also have had some means of locomotion or they could not have accompanied free competition.

> Meantime the markets kept ever growing, the demand ever rising. Even manufacture no longer sufficed. Thereupon, steam and machinery revolutionized industrial production. The place of manufacture was taken by the giant, Modern Industry . . . (*Communist Manifesto*, p. 322.)

Markets were not enlarged by men—they grew. Industrial production was not revolutionized by men using steam and machinery, but steam and machinery themselves revolutionized industrial production. Modern Industry is called a "giant" and is said to have moved in and taken the place of manufacture.

At another point modern industry is said to have had a "stormy youth." (*Capital*, Vol. I, p. 608.) In another passage it is found to be "advancing" and "developing."

> The advance of industry, whose involuntary promoter is the bourgeoisie, replaces the isolation of the laborers, due to competition, by their involuntary combination, due to association. The development of Modern Industry, therefore, cuts from under its feet the very foundation on which the bourgeoisie produces and appropriates products. (*Communist Manifesto*, p. 334.)

In this passage the bourgeoisie is given feet. Industry, in another, is given a face.

> Of all the classes that stand face to face with the bourgeoisie to-day the proletariat alone is a really revolutionary class. The other classes decay and finally disappear in the face of modern industry; the proletariat is its special and essential product. (*Communist Manifesto*, pp. 331-332.)

At another point the proletariat is given a "great heart."

> Workingmen's Paris, with its Commune, will be forever celebrated as the glorious harbinger of a new society. Its martyrs are enshrined in the great heart of the working class. (Marx, *Civil War in France*, p. 429.)

Marx and Engels' frequent use of birth and pregnancy metaphors indicates that they habitually thought in terms of analogy from organic life.

> The France of today was ready-made within the womb of the Parliamentary republic. All that was wanted was a bayonet thrust, in order that the bubble

burst, and the monster leap forth to sight. (Marx, *Eighteenth Brumaire of Louis Napoleon*, p. 139.)

What we have to deal with here is a communist society, not as if it had *developed on a basis of its own*, but on the contrary as *it emerges from capitalist society*, which is thus in every respect tainted economically, morally and intellectually with the hereditary disease of the old society from whose womb it is emerging. (Marx, *Critique of the Gotha Program*, p. 29.)

The working class did not expect miracles from the Commune. They have no ready-made utopias to introduce *par decret du peuple*. . . . They have no ideals to realize, but to set free the elements of the new society with which old collapsing bourgeois society itself is pregnant. (Marx, *Civil War in France*, p. 408.)

The feudal middle ages also developed in its womb the class which was destined in the future course of its evolution to be the standard-bearer of the modern demand for equality: the bourgeoisie. (*Anti-Duhring*, p. 120.)

As is well known, however, from the moment when, like a butterfly from the chrysalis, the bourgeoisie arose out of the burghers of the feudal period . . . it was always and inevitably accompanied by its shadow, the proletariat. (*Ibid.*, p. 122.)

The proletariat goes through various stages of development. With its birth begins its struggle with the bourgeoisie. (*Communist Manifesto*, p. 329.)

After the birth of the proletariat, depicted in the quotation immediately above, it begins to grow in strength.

But with the development of industry the proletariat not only increases in number; it becomes concentrated in greater masses, its strength grows and it feels that strength more. (*Communist Manifesto*, p. 330.)

The image is that of a young man beginning to flex his muscles. Not only does the proletariat increase in strength, it feels that increase. Feeling, in other words, is attributed to this entity.

Metaphorical expressions and analogies from organic life are frequently used by writers as a shorthand method of describing complex processes. The significant point is, however, that in the writings of Marx and Engels the metaphors and analogies are not shorthand but are the descriptions themselves. No complex processes are thought to be involved. Simple visual images are used to describe intricate historical changes involving millions of persons and extending over several centuries.

> From the serfs of the middle ages sprang the chartered burghers of the earliest towns. (*Communist Manifesto*, p. 322.)

> The modern bourgeois society that has sprouted from the ruins of feudal society . . . (*Ibid.*)

> Modern industry has established the world market . . . (*Ibid.*)

> . . . the bourgeoisie developed, increased its capital, and pushed into the background every class handed down from the Middle Ages. (*Ibid.*, p. 323.)

> The weapons with which the bourgeoisie felled feudalism to the ground are now turned against the bourgeoisie itself.

> But not only has the bourgeoisie forged the weapons that bring death to itself: it has also called into existence the men who are to wield those weapons— the modern working class—the proletarians. (*Ibid.*, pp. 327-28.)

All the passages thus far examined in this appendix have one important feature in common: they attribute the quality of life or self-propulsion to the entities dealt with. Whether it be modern industry "advancing," free competition "stepping," the forces of production "rebelling," the chartered burghers "springing," modern bourgeois society "sprouting," or the bourgeoisie "pushing," or "forging," the self-movement or self-development is there. This mode of thinking enormously simplifies the problem of dealing with historical change. In the pages from which the following passages are taken, for example, Marx and Engels explain virtually every important development of the preceding century by attributing it to one of their great self-propelled entities, "the bourgeoisie."

The need of a constantly expanding market for its products chases the bourgeoisie over the whole surface of the globe. It must nestle everywhere, settle everywhere, establish connections everywhere.

The bourgeoisie has through its exploitation of the world-market given a cosmopolitan character to production and consumption in every country. To the great chagrin of reactionists, it has drawn from under the feet of industry the national ground on which it stood. (*Communist Manifesto*, pp. 324-325.)

The bourgeoisie has subjected the country to the rule of the towns. It has created enormous cities, has greatly increased the urban population as compared with the rural . . . (*Ibid.*, p. 325.)

The bourgeoisie keeps more and more doing away with the scattered state of the population, of the means of production, and of property. It has agglomerated population, centralized means of production, and has concentrated property in a few hands . . .

The bourgeoisie, during its rule of scarce one hundred years, has created more massive and more colossal productive forces than have all preceding generations together. Subjection of Nature's forces to man, machinery, application of chemistry to industry and agriculture, steam-navigation, railways, electric telegraphs, clearing of whole continents for cultivation, canalization of rivers, whole populations conjured out of the ground—what earlier century had even a presentiment that such productive forces slumbered in the lap of social labor? (*Ibid.*, p. 326.)

Having catalogued the social, political and economic changes of the preceding epoch, Marx and Engels, with a single sweep, "explain" them by stating that they are the work of "the bourgeoisie." By the simple expedient of investing this abstraction with the power of self-movement, Marx and Engels manage to create the illusion of causation.

The causation found in the Marxian system is not genuine causation but is simply the sort of logical necessitation found in the Hegelian system. Physical causation and logical necessity were identified in Marx's mind and treated as equivalents.

. . . Both for the production on a mass scale of this communist consciousness, and for the success of the cause itself, the alteration of men on a mass scale is necessary, an alteration which can only take place in a practical movement, a *revolution*; this revolution is necessary, therefore, not only because the ruling class cannot be overthrown in any other way, but also because the class *overthrowing* it can only in a revolution succeed in ridding itself of all the muck of ages and become fitted to found society anew. (Marx, *German Ideology*, p. 69.)

The revolution is "necessary," according to this passage, because only by means of a revolution can the ruling class be overthrown and the overthrowing class become fit to found a new society. The revolution is necessary, not in the sense that it is physically unavoidable, but in the sense that it is the indispensable condition for the achievement of Marx's desires. Marx writes as if he has shown the inevitability of revolution whereas he has actually only stated that it is desirable. He attempts to argue from "necessity," in the sense of an indispensable condition, to "necessity," in the sense of physical causation, and thus to invest his system with the physical basis which it lacks. This line of reasoning is found time and again.

> By more and more transforming the great majority of the population into proletarians, the capitalist mode of production brings into being the force which, under penalty of its own destruction, is compelled to carry out this revolution. (*Anti-Duhring*, p. 314.)

Engels states that the proletariat is "compelled" to carry out this revolution. What compels it? There is no physical compulsion but only the conditional statement that if the proletariat desires to survive then it must revolt.

> In other words, it is because both the productive forces created by the modern capitalist mode of production and also the system of distribution of goods established by it have come into burning contradiction with that mode of production itself, and in fact to such a degree that, if the whole of modern society is not to perish, a revolution of the mode of production and distribution must take place, a revolution which will put an end to all class divisions. On this tangible, material fact . . . modern socialism's confidence of victory is founded. (*Anti-Duhring*, p. 179.)

Having demonstrated, to his own satisfaction, that a revolution in the mode of production is an indispensable means to a desired end, Engels rests confident in his belief that this revolution will come to pass. Having demonstrated its logical necessity he assumes that he has demonstrated its physical necessity as well.

The explanation for these peculiarities in the writing of Marx and Engels lies in the fact that they habitually thought in terms of immanent causation rather than in terms of external or mechanical causation. For Marx and Engels, the explanation of any event is to be found in the inherent characteristics of the entities involved rather than in the nature and strength of the external forces acting on the situation. This is not surprising in view of the fact that Marx and Engels "started out" from the Hegelian dialectic, from the system which has at its heart the conception of self-development. Instead of Hegel's Idea developing dialectically, however, for Marx and Engels it is nature and human history. Immanence is to be found everywhere in the Marxian system because Marx and Engels believed that the universe and everything in it developed according to immanent dialectical laws. "Dialectics is nothing more than the science of the general laws of motion and development of Nature, human society and thought." (*Anti-Duhring*, p. 160.)

Since Marx and Engels were convinced that it was the nature of the universe to develop dialectically, the causation, the dynamic principle in their system is simply the "necessity" that all things in nature and human history have of acting "in obedience to dialectical forms." This is the engine in the Marxian scheme and the only engine.

Hitherto every form of society has been based . . . on the antagonism of oppressing and oppressed classes. But in order to oppress a class, certain conditions must be assured to it under which it can, at least, continue its slavish existence. The serf, in the period of serf-dom, raised himself to membership in the commune, just as the petty bourgeois, under the yoke of feudal absolutism, managed to develop into a bourgeois. The modern laborer, on the contrary, instead of rising with the progress of industry, sinks deeper and deeper below the conditions of existence of his own class. He becomes a pauper, and pauperism develops more rapidly than population and wealth. And here it becomes evident that the bourgeoisie is unfit any longer to be the ruling class in society, and to impose its conditions of existence upon society as an over-riding law. It is unfit to rule because it is incompetent to assure an existence to its slave within his slavery, because it cannot help letting him sink into such a state that it has to feed him, instead of being fed by him. Society can no longer live under this bourgeoisie; in other words, its existence is no longer compatible with society. (*Communist Manifesto*, p. 333.)

Because the bourgeoisie can no longer see to it that the oppressed class continues to exist, it is declared "unfit" to rule. Society can no longer live under the bourgeoisie. Its continued existence is "no longer compatible" with society. The implication is that since the bourgeoisie is no longer compatible with society, it (the bourgeoisie) must disappear. Focusing mĕrely on the logical structure of the argument, it is necessary to ask why it is the bourgeoisie that is to disappear. If the bourgeoisie can no longer provide the conditions of existence for its slave, why is it not the slave that is to perish? Only the unspoken major premise, the assumption that all things behave dialectically, dooms the bourgeoisie. Since Marx and Engels regard the bourgeoisie as the thesis and the proletariat as the antithesis, the conclusion of the syllogism is that the bourgeoisie must give way to the proletariat, the thesis to the antithesis. Take away this major premise, take away the assumption that all things follow a three phase dialectical rhythm, and the Marxian universe, denuded of its iron laws, grinds to a halt.

The capitalist mode of appropriation, the result of the capitalist mode of production, produces capitalist private property. This is the first negation of individual private property, as founded on the labour of the proprietor. But capitalist production begets, with the inexorability of a law of Nature, its own negation. It is the negation of the negation. (*Capital*, Vol. I, p. 837.)

Marx's assurance that capitalist private property will be "negated" rests solely on his belief that the dialectic cannot stop with a single negation but must continue to the "negation of the negation."

We see then: the means of production and of exchange on whose foundation the bourgeoisie built itself up, were generated in feudal society. At a certain stage in the development of these means of production and of exchange, the conditions under which feudal society produced and exchanged, the feudal organisation of agriculture and manufacturing industry, in one word, the feudal relations of property became no longer compatible with the already developed productive forces; they became so many fetters. They had to burst asunder; they were burst asunder. (*Communist Manifesto*, pp. 326-27.)

Because the feudal relations of property became fetters on the productive forces they were forced to burst asunder. Why? What caused them to burst asunder? They had to burst asunder because they were "no longer compatible," with their antithesis, the productive forces, and because the thesis always gives way to the antithesis in our dialectical universe.

Those who accept the dialectic as the ruling principle of the universe find causation aplenty in these passages and in the Marxian scheme as a whole and find that Marx did indeed uncover "tendencies working with iron necessity towards inevitable results." (Marx, Preface to the first edition of *Capital*.) Those who reject this faith find the Marxian system bereft of necessity and inevitability.*

---

*So far as I know, Max Eastman is the only writer on this subject to understand the significance of the point. The following is one of several passages from *Marx and Lenin* stressing the matter: "Disregarding the empirical analysis of capitalism in this passage—the formulation of historic and contemporary facts—ask only where is located, or whence derived, the dynamic force which gives certainty of the motion into the future of this self-contradictory institution. That dynamic force is simply not to be found. Unless you have already the habit of assuming that all that group of facts denoted by the general term "mode of production" are destined by a mystical necessity evolve upward, you find no reason here why the shell of capitalism should inevitably burst. . . . In this book as elsewhere, it is by conceiving the class struggle as a contradiction between two generalizations—the capitalist force of production and the capitalist production-relations—and inferring the victory of the proletariat as a logical conclusion according to the Hegelian system, that Marx arrives at that "iron necessity" of socialism, which is supposed to rest upon the overwhelming assemblage and analysis of facts in Das Kapital." Eastman, Max. *Marx and Lenin*. New York: Albert and Charles Boni, 1927, pp. 102-103.

BIBLIOGRAPHY

A. WRITINGS OF KARL MARX

Capital. Ed. Friedrich Engels. New York: The Modern Library, n. d. (Copyright 1906 by Charles H. Kerr & Co.)

Capital, The Communist Manifesto and Other Writings by Karl Marx. Ed. Max Eastman. New York: The Modern Library, 1932.

The Civil War in France. Reprinted in *Capital, The Communist Manifesto and Other Writings by Karl Marx.* Ed. Max Eastman. New York: The Modern Library, 1932.

The Class Struggles in France 1848-1850. London: Lawrence and Wishart, 1936.

A Contribution to the Critique of Political Economy. Tr. N. I. Stone. New York: The International Library Publishing Co., 1904.

Critique of the Gotha Program. New York: International Publishers, 1933.

The Eighteenth Brumaire of Louis Bonaparte. Tr. Daniel de Leon. Chicago: C. H. Kerr and Co., 1914.

Poverty of Philosophy. Ed. C. P. Dutt and V. Chattopadhyaya. (Contains Engels' Preface to the First German Edition; Engels' Preface to the Second German Edition. Also Appendix containing Engels' Introduction to the *Address on the Question of Free Trade* and Marx's *Address on the Question of Free Trade*.) New York: International Publishers, n. d.

Preface to *A Contribution to the Critique of Political Economy.* Reprinted in *Selected Works.* 2nd English edition. Ed. I. B. Lasker. Moscow: Foreign Languages Publishing House, 1946. 2 vols.

Selected Essays. Tr. H. J. Stenning. London: Leonard Parsons, 1926.

Theses on Feuerbach. Reprinted in *Selected Works.* Moscow: Foreign Languages Publishing House, 1946.

Value, Price and Profit. Reprinted in *Selected Works.* Moscow: Foreign Languages Publishing House, 1946.

Wage-Labour and Capital. Reprinted in *Selected Works*. Moscow: Foreign Languages Publishing House, 1946.

B. WRITINGS OF FRIEDRICH ENGELS

The Condition of the Working Class in England in 1844. Tr. Florence Kelly Wischnewetsky. London: G. Allen & Unwin, Ltd., 1926.

Dialectics and Nature. Tr. and ed. Clemens Dutt. New York: International Publishers, 1940.

Germany: Revolution and Counter-Revolution. New York: International Publishers, 1933.

Herr Eugen Duhring's Revolution in Science. Tr. Emile Burns. Ed. C. P. Dutt. New York: International Publishers. Printed in the U.S.S.R.: Glavlit B-62552, n. d.

History of the Communist League. New York: International Publishers, 1933.

Introduction to the German Edition of *The Civil War in France*. Reprinted in *Capital, The Communist Manifesto and Other Writings by Karl Marx*. New York: The Modern Library, 1932.

Ludwig Feuerbach and the Outcome of Classical German Philosophy. Reprinted in Karl Marx, *Selected Works*. 2nd English edition. Ed. I. B. Lasker. Moscow: Foreign Languages Publishing House, 1946. 2 vols.

The Origin of the Family, Private Property and the State. Tr. Ernest Untermann. Chicago: C. H. Kerr and Co., 1902.

The Peasant War in Germany. London: G. Allen & Unwin, Ltd., 1927.

Socialism, Utopian and Scientific. Tr. Edward Aveling. Chicago: C. H. Kerr and Co., 1908.

C. JOINT WRITINGS OF KARL MARX AND FRIEDRICH ENGELS

The Communist Manifesto. Reprinted in *Capital, The Communist Manifesto and Other Writings by Karl Marx*. Ed. Max Eastman. New York: The Modern Library, 1932.

The German Ideology, Parts I and III. New York: International Publishers, 1939.

Selected Correspondence. New York: International Publishers, 1934.

D. WRITINGS OF V. I. LENIN

Collected Works. New York: International Publishers, various dates. 36 vols. (when completed).

BIBLIOGRAPHY

Essentials of Lenin. London: Lawrence and Wishart, 1947. 2 vols.

Marx-Engels Marxism. New York: International Publishers, 1931.

Materialism and Empirio-Criticism. New York: International Publishers, 1927.

Selected Works. Translated from the Russian as issued by the Marx-Engels-Lenin Institute. New York: International Publishers, various dates. 12 vols.

E. WRITINGS OF JOSEPH STALIN

From Socialism to Communism in the Soviet Union. Report on the Work of the Central Committee to the Eighteenth Congress of the C.P.S.U. (B). New York: International Publishers, 1939.

The Great Patriotic War of the Soviet Union. New York: International Publishers, 1945.

Leninism. Tr. Eden and Cedar Paul. New York: International Publishers, 1928 and 1933. 2 vols.

Marxism and the National Question. New York: International Publishers, 1942.

War Speeches, Orders of the Day and Answers to Foreign Press Correspondents During the Great Patriotic War. London: Hutchinson and Co., Ltd., n. d.

F. OTHER

Commission of the Central Committee of the C.P.S.U. *History of the Communist Party of the Soviet Union*. (Authorized by the Central Committee of the C.P.S.U. (B). New York: International Publishers, 1939.

Stalin, Molotov, Kaganovitch and Others. *Socialism Victorious*. Speeches delivered at the 17th Congress of the C.P.S.U. New York: International Publishers, 1935.

Secondary Sources

EASTMAN, MAX. *Marx and Lenin*. New York: Albert and Charles Boni, 1927.

FINER, HERMAN. *Mussolini's Italy*. New York: Henry Holt and Company, 1935.

ROUSSEAU, JEAN JACQUES. *Confessions*. New York: The Modern Library, n. d.

——. *The Social Contract and Discourses*. Tr. G. D. H. Cole. London: J. M. Dent & Sons, Ltd., 1946.

Index

INDEX